BASED ON
THE CLASSIC
BEST-SELLER

YOUR SPIRITUAL GIFTS

CAN HELP YOUR CHURCH GROW

GROUP STUDY GUIDE

C. PETER WAGNER

LARRY KEEFAUVER, EDITOR

Gospel Light

YOUR SPIRITUAL GIFTS CAN HELP YOUR CHURCH GROW

Gospel Light is an evangelical Christian publisher dedicated to serving the local church. We believe God's vision for Gospel Light is to provide church leaders with biblical, user-friendly materials that will help them evangelize, disciple and minister to children, youth and families.

We hope this Gospel Light resource will help you discover biblical truth for your own life and help you minister to adults. God bless you in your work.

For a free catalog from Gospel Light please contact your Christian supplier or call 1-800-4-GOSPEL.

PUBLISHING STAFF
Jean Daly, Editor
Kyle Duncan, Editorial Director
Gary S. Greig, Ph.D., Vice President, Editor in Chief
Carolyn Thomas, Designer

ISBN 0-8307-1758-7

How to Make Clean Copies from This Book

You may make copies of portions of this book with a clean conscience if:

* you (or someone in your organization) are the original purchaser;
* you are using the copies you make for a noncommercial purpose (such as teaching or promoting your ministry) within your church or organization;
* you follow the instructions provided in this book.

However, it is ILLEGAL for you to make copies if:

* you are using the material to promote, advertise or sell a product or service other than for ministry fund-raising;
* you are using the material in or on a product for sale;
* you or your organization are **not** the original purchaser of this book.

By following these guidelines you help us keep our products affordable.

Thank you,

Gospel Light

Contents

YOUR SPIRITUAL
GIFTS CAN
HELP YOUR
CHURCH GROW

How to Use the Group Study Guide and the Regal Book *Your Spiritual Gifts Can Help Your Church Grow*

This group study guide is a streamlined and effective tool for leading your small group or Sunday School class through a meaningful study of the Bible course *Your Spiritual Gifts Can Help Your Church Grow.*

Group Study Guide

The text that accompanies this study is the Regal book *Your Spiritual Gifts Can Help Your Church Grow* by C. Peter Wagner. Because this group study guide does not include the complete text on spiritual gifts, it is imperative that each leader/teacher secures a copy of the book *Your Spiritual Gifts Can Help Your Church Grow* in order to teach this course.

Regal Book

The book *Your Spiritual Gifts Can Help Your Church Grow* is so vital to the study of spiritual gifts that you should see that each of your group members has a personal copy. Only then will he or she receive the full advantage of this study. Several ways to make the book available to members include: (1) members buy personal copies; (2) church supplies copies; (3) church and individuals share costs.

Wagner-Modified Houts Questionnaire

The Wagner-Modified Houts Questionnaire helps group members determine their spiritual gifts. As a part of Session 12, students will complete the survey to gain a greater understanding of how God has gifted them, and how to use those gifts to help their church grow. You may reproduce this questionnaire for classroom use only.

THE REDISCOVERY OF SPIRITUAL GIFTS

SESSION KEYS

Key Verse

"There are different kinds of gifts, but the same Spirit. Now to each one the manifestation of the Spirit is given for the common good." 1 Corinthians 12:4,7

Key Idea

The gifts of the Holy Spirit have been rediscovered by many churches in the last two decades prompting many Christians to have a renewed interest in the work and gifts of the Holy Spirit.

Key Resources

* Chapter 1 of the book *Your Spiritual Gifts Can Help Your Church Grow*
* Copies of the Session 1 handout, "Meet the Holy Spirit"

Preparation

* Provide name tags and pencils or pens for everyone in the group.
* If you select Choice 1 under Getting Started, have a box gift wrapped and placed in another box that is also gift wrapped.
* If you select Choice 2 under Getting Started, prepare adhesive labels that you can put on people's backs. Each adhesive label has one of the following talents or skills listed on it: Plays tennis, Plays basketball, Plays football, Cooks, Writes novels, Sings solos, Plays the piano, Sews, Speaks in public, Sculpts, Knits, Ice-skates, Paints, Decorates rooms, Snow-skis, Plays chess, Races cars, Juggles. If there are more people in your group than talents or skills on this list, make up some of your own or duplicate adhesive labels.
* Have extra pencils and paper for group members. You will also need access to a chalkboard, newsprint and felt-tip pens, or an overhead projector for all of these sessions.

Session 1 at a Glance

SECTION	60-MINUTE SESSION	90-MINUTE SESSION	ACTIVITY
Getting Started	**10 Minutes**	**20 Minutes**	
Choice 1 *or*	10 Minutes	10 Minutes	What's a Gift? *or*
Choice 2			Discover a Gift
Option		10 Minutes	Spirit-Given Gifts
Getting into the Word	**45 Minutes**	**65 Minutes**	
Step 1	20 Minutes	20 Minutes	Meet the Holy Spirit
Step 2	25 Minutes	25 Minutes	The Holy Spirit in History
Option		20 Minutes	Discover Spiritual Gifts
Getting Personal	**5 Minutes**	**5 Minutes**	
	5 Minutes	5 Minutes	Gifts that Have Encouraged

S E S S I O N   P L A N

Leader's Choice

60- and 90-minute meeting options: This session is designed to be completed in one 60-minute meeting. If you want to extend the session to a 90-minute meeting, refer to the boxes marked with the clock symbol. These options will provide additional learning experiences expanding the session to 90 minutes.

Getting Started (10 Minutes)

Choice 1—What's a Gift?

Before anyone arrives place your wrapped gift on a table in front of the room in full view of all the group members. Welcome people as they arrive and give each person a name tag. Ask each person to find a partner. Invite them to share with one another:

✳ **What was your favorite Christmas?**
✳ **What was one of the best gifts you ever received?**
✳ **What is the best gift you ever gave?**

Point out the gift in front of the room. Explain: **The triune God gives so much to us. God, the Father, gave us Creation and His Son, Jesus. God, the Son, gave His life for us on the cross and gives us eternal life. Jesus also gives us a very precious gift that fulfills His promise in Matthew 28:20, "I am with you always." What is that ever-present gift that we might represent by this gift on the table?**

Have the group suggest whatever comes to mind and list it on a chalkboard, newsprint or overhead projector. One answer you are looking for is "The Holy Spirit." When that answer is suggested, ask everyone to turn to Acts 2:38 and silently read it with you.

Now the Bible tells us that as believers we receive the gift of the Holy Spirit. Not only that, but there's more. If this wrapped gift represents the gift of the

Holy Spirit, then what might be inside this gift? Spend a few moments allowing the group to guess what they think might be inside of the gift. Then open the gift revealing the second gift inside. **The Bible also teaches that the Holy Spirit gives gifts. Just as the Father and the Son give, so the Spirit gives gifts. In this study we shall be exploring what those gifts are, how they minister within the Body of Christ and what particular gifts the Holy Spirit has given to each of you.**

Choice 2—Discover a Gift

Welcome everyone as they arrive and give each person a name tag for his or her own name. Put one of the talent or skill adhesive labels on each person's back. Give these instructions:

On your back is a talent or skill. You are to go around to everyone in the room and introduce yourself. Then you may ask each person you meet one question about the skill or talent listed on your back. That question must be able to be answered with a simple *yes* **or** *no.* **Try to guess the talent or skill written on your back.**

After each person has guessed what's written on his or her label, discuss in the group:

✳ **How would you define a skill or a talent?** A talent or skill is a natural ability that can be refined or increased with practice and increased knowledge.

✳ **How is a skill or talent different from a spiritual gift?** A spiritual gift from God is not natural, not something we are born with or can earn or increase with natural knowledge or practice. While God gives both talents and spiritual gifts, talents exist in the natural while spiritual gifts are in the supernatural.

In our study together, we will be exploring spiritual gifts given to us by God through the Holy Spirit. These gifts are not earned, nor are they natural skills or talents. They are spiritual gifts freely given by the grace of the Holy Spirit.

....

Getting Started Option (10 Minutes)

Spirit-Given Gifts

This option will add 10 minutes to either one of the Getting Started choices.

Ask everyone to get with a partner and sit down facing the partner. Make certain that everyone has a pencil and piece of paper. Tell the pairs that they have five minutes to try to list as many spiritual gifts from the Holy Spirit as they can. Call time and then invite the pairs to call out the names of spiritual gifts on their lists. Write those gifts on the chalkboard.

There are many spiritual gifts listed in the New Testament. The Holy Spirit gives these gifts for ministry within the Body of Christ. You have remembered many of them. However, some of them you have not listed and some that you listed are not formally mentioned in the Bible. We will study in depth many of the gifts of the Holy Spirit as they are listed and described in the New Testament.

....

Getting into the Word (45 Minutes)

Step 1—Meet the Holy Spirit (20 Minutes)

Give everyone a copy of the Session 1 handout, "Meet the Holy Spirit." With their partners, ask them to complete the sheets together. Tell them they have 15 minutes to complete their sheets.

Step 2—The Holy Spirit in History (25 Minutes)

Read pages 13-19 in *Your Spiritual Gifts Can Help Your Church Grow.* Summarize what has happened historically as described by Peter Wagner. Be certain your summary includes these key points:

✳ **The Holy Spirit moved powerfully in the Early Church as we read in the book of Acts.**

* The Holy Spirit was affirmed in all the creeds of the Early Church.
* Interest in the Holy Spirit and His gifts waned in church history.
* A renewed interest in the Holy Spirit emerged in the early 1900s.
* Some intellectuals believed that the gifts of the Spirit ceased after the apostles died.
* Church leaders throughout history have mentioned the Holy Spirit and His work. Note the influences of Justin Martyr, Irenaeus, Bishop Hilary, Augustine, Thomas Aquinas, Martin Luther, John Calvin, John Owen and John Wesley.
* A renewed interest in the work of the Holy Spirit and spiritual gifts emerged in the '70s.
* Churches and denominations have become increasingly open and interested in spiritual gifts for the ministry and priesthood of all believers. Describe the difference between the priesthood of all believers and the ministry of all believers.

Share your summary with the group in about five to seven minutes. After your summary, as a group discuss:

* What are your beliefs about the ministry of all believers?
* How would your church respond to the ministry of spiritual gifts?
* What is your personal experience of spiritual gifts?

Getting into the Word Option (20 Minutes)
Discover Spiritual Gifts

This option will add 20 minutes to the Getting into the Word section.

Divide your group into three small groups. On the chalkboard or overhead write these three Scripture references: Romans 12:3-8; 1 Corinthians 12:1-11; Ephesians 4:1-16. Assign each group one of these Scripture passages.

Ask each group to make a list of all the spiritual gifts they find mentioned in their assigned passage. Give the groups five minutes to compile their lists.

As a group, list on the board all the gifts that have been discovered. As a group, try to combine the three lists into one, only listing once any gift that may be mentioned in more than one passage.

Then give everyone in the group three votes. Read aloud the list and ask group members to vote for the three gifts they have seen most active in your church. Circle the three gifts that received the most votes. Discuss:

* Why are these gifts so prevalent in our church?
* Look at the gifts that received the least votes. Why are these gifts not active in our church?
* Which gifts on the list do people in your group understand the least? Which would they like to learn more about?

Getting Personal (5 Minutes)
Gifts that Have Encouraged

Ask each person in the group to think of someone he or she knows that may be a pastor, teacher, family member or Christian friend who has really ministered to his or her life through the power of the Holy Spirit. That person may have been gifted in encouragement, faith or teaching. Then say to the group: **Think of one gift from the Holy Spirit that you have seen in the life of another Christian who has ministered to you. Get back with partners and share one gift of the Holy Spirit that has ministered to you.**

Now pray for one another a prayer something like this: "Holy Spirit, comfort, counsel, guide and teach (name) during the coming week. In Jesus' name. Amen."

IGNORANCE IS NOT BLISS

S E S S I O N   K E Y S

Key Verses

"We have different gifts, according to the grace given us." Romans 12:6
"But to each one of us grace has been given as Christ apportioned it." Ephesians 4:7

Key Idea

The most basic step for a Christian in discovering God's plan for life is to discover his or her spiritual gift or gifts.

Key Resources

* Chapter 2 of the book *Your Spiritual Gifts Can Help Your Church Grow*
* Copies of the Session 2 handout, "Calling, Gifts and Warning"

Preparation

* If you select Choice 1 under Getting Started, make up sets of four 3x5-inch cards. Each set has one card with one of the following body parts written on it: Head, Arms, Torso, Legs. Stack these sets on top of one another so that you may give them out equally as people enter the room. If your group does not divide up evenly in groups of four, the last two or three people who enter the room can be given an extra card to complete a whole set.
* If you select Choice 2 under Getting Started, list on a piece of newsprint or poster board all 27 gifts listed in the directory immediately following the contents of *Your Spiritual Gifts Can Help Your Church Grow*.
* Have extra Bibles, paper and pencils for your group.

SECTION	60-MINUTE SESSION	90-MINUTE SESSION	ACTIVITY
GETTING STARTED	**15 MINUTES**	**25 MINUTES**	
Choice 1 *or*	15 Minutes	15 Minutes	All Part of the Same Body *or*
Choice 2			Ignorance Is Not Bliss!
Option		10 Minutes	What I Know About Gifts
GETTING INTO THE WORD	**40 MINUTES**	**60 MINUTES**	
Step 1	20 Minutes	20 Minutes	God's Will and His Gifts
Step 2	20 Minutes	20 Minutes	Calling, Gifts and Warning
Option		20 Minutes	Gift Benefits
GETTING PERSONAL	**5 MINUTES**	**5 MINUTES**	
	5 Minutes	5 Minutes	Knowing the Gifts

S E S S I O N   P L A N

Leader's Choice

60- and 90-minute meeting options: This session is designed to be completed in one 60-minute meeting. If you want to extend the session to a 90-minute meeting, refer to the boxes marked with the clock symbol. These options will provide additional learning experiences expanding the session to 90 minutes.

Getting Started (15 Minutes)

Choice 1—All Part of the Same Body

As everyone arrives, greet the group members and hand each a body-part card. Tell them to find three other people each with different parts of the body. Then as a group of four, ask them to sit together in a circle. After everyone is in a group of four, say: **Before we start our study, take a moment to go around your circle and introduce yourself. Share one blessing from the Lord that you have received this past week. Take about five minutes for this.**

Every part of the body is important. All parts are necessary for the body to be whole and complete. This is what Paul writes about in 1 Corinthians 12 and Romans 12. Briefly discuss in your small group what your body would be like without your part. Start with the person who is tallest and go around to the right. You have two minutes for this. Go! Pause.

The Body of Christ has many parts. Think of someone in our church whose gift from the Lord means much to you. Imagine what it would be like without that person and his or her gift in our church. Without revealing the name of

that person and his or her gift, share with your small group the feeling and loss you would have if that gift were missing from our church. Start with the person who went last and go around to the right. You have four minutes to share.

Choice 2—Ignorance Is Not Bliss!

Immediately following the contents of *Your Spiritual Gifts Can Help Your Church Grow* is a list of the 27 gifts discussed in the book. Use this list as your reference. Greet everyone as they arrive and put them into groups of four. After everyone has arrived, give these directions: **In the book we are studying, *Your Spiritual Gifts Can Help Your Church Grow*, there are 27 spiritual gifts listed from the Bible. First Corinthians 12 begins by saying "Now about spiritual gifts, brothers, I do not want you to be ignorant." As a small group, introduce yourselves to one another and share one blessing you received this past week from the Lord. Then try to list as many gifts as you can think of from Scripture. You have about eight minutes for this.** Pause. At the end of this sharing time, put up a list of the 27 gifts on newsprint or poster board in front of the group.

Now compare this list with your group's list of gifts. **How many of them did you know? How many of them didn't you know. That is your "ignorance" index.** As a small group discuss briefly:

✳ **Which gifts on Peter Wagner's list have you never heard of before?**

✳ **Which three gifts are most active in our church? Which three are the least active?**

• •

Getting Started Option (10 Minutes)

What I Know About Gifts

This option will add 10 minutes to either one of the Getting Started choices.

Write these sentences on the board:

✳ **One spiritual gift I know a lot about is:**

✳ **One spiritual gift I am ignorant about is:**

Explain both responses.

In your small groups of four, go around the circle starting with the person who got up earliest this morning, and share the completion to these sentences I have written on the board. Take about two minutes each to share.

• •

Getting into the Word (40 Minutes)

Step 1— God's Will and His Gifts (20 Minutes)

Have everyone read Romans 12:1-6 silently while you read it to the group. Write on the chalkboard or overhead: "His good, pleasing and perfect will" and "we have different gifts, according to the grace given us."

Share with the group: **God gives gifts and power to each of us through His Spirit. These gifts accomplish His will in our lives and allow us to minister to one another in the Body of Christ. Dr. Wagner states that there is a difference between "Consecration Theology" and "Gift Theology." Briefly summarized, "Consecration Theology" says that if we just love God enough we should be able to do anything He wills for us. On the other hand, "Gift Theology" recognizes that God gives different gifts to different people. While all of us may not be able to do His will with supernatural faith, some of us will have that gift. While not all of us can be wonderful teachers of God's Word, some will have that gift. "Consecration**

Theology" would say that if you can't teach, give or believe like some in the Body of Christ then you should feel guilty and try harder. "Gift Theology" would say that God has given all of us differing gifts as He wills to complete our church. So those gifted in supernatural faith can encourage others while they are taught by those with the gift of teaching. All of us then need one another's gifts in order to realize God's will for all of our lives. As a total group let's discuss:

✳ **What don't you understand about "Gift Theology" or "Consecration Theology"?**
✳ **How would you further agree or disagree with what Dr. Wagner is saying?**

Step 2—Calling, Gifts and Warning (20 Minutes)

Give everyone in the group a copy of Session 2 handout, "Calling, Gifts and Warning." Ask each person in his or her group of four to complete the handout in about 10 minutes. Then explain that you will call time and give them instructions on what to share in their groups of four. After everyone has completed the handout, give these instructions:

1. **Share how you answered Part One in your groups.**
2. **Now share how you answered Part Two.**
3. **Now share how you answered Part Three.**

As a total group discuss:

✳ **How can our church use God's gifts for us and still avoid the pitfalls?**

Share some of the abuses of gifts from pages 45-48 of the text.

✳ **How can we guard against these abuses?**

Getting into the Word Option (20 Minutes)
Gift Benefits

This option will add 20 minutes to the Getting into the Word section.

In small groups of four people each, give every group the assignment to look up the passages you list on the board. Then have group members write on the backs of their handout sheets at least three biblical benefits from spiritual gifts within the context of the Body of Christ. List these passages on the board: 1 Corinthians 12:16; Ephesians 4:13; 1 Peter 4:10-11.

In the small groups, invite them to discuss how the benefits they listed on their handouts compare with the list of biblical benefits they just compiled.

Now ask the small groups to look up 1 Corinthians 4:2 and Matthew 25:14-30.

As a total group discuss:

✳ **How can we be good and faithful stewards of the gifts that God has given us?**

Getting Personal (5 Minutes)
Knowing the Gifts

In the small groups of four people each, ask each person in the circle to share:

✳ **One concern about spiritual gifts that I have is:**
✳ **One thing I learned about gifts is:**
✳ **One way our church could benefit from spiritual gifts is:**

Once all the groups have shared, join as a total group in a circle. Lead a corporate prayer: **Silently pray and thank the Lord for the person on your right and the gift or gifts they have received through the Holy Spirit. Now pray the same way for the person on your left. Lord Jesus, I thank you for sending your Holy Spirit and giving gifts to Your Body that we might fulfill Your will and ministry in our church. Give us the wisdom to avoid all abuses and a desire to seek after Your gifts. In Jesus' name. Amen.**

Calling, Gifts and Warning

Part One

Read 1 Corinthians 12:1-27; Galatians 3:26-29; Philippians 2:1-11 and 1 Peter 4:10.

Answer the following statements *True* or *False* by circling your belief. Then check your answer with the Scripture reference.

True   False   1. Every Christian is given at least one gift and possibly more.
(See 1 Corinthians 12:7; 1 Peter 4:10.)

True   False   2. Women are equally gifted with men in the Body of Christ.
(See 1 Corinthians 12:7; Galatians 3:26-29.)

True   False   3. All Christians have a general calling on their lives to be servants.
(See Matthew 20:26; Philippians 2:1-11.)

True   False   4. Every Christian has a specific ministry of serving in the Body
of Christ by using the gift God has given him or her.
(See 1 Corinthians 12:21-27.)

Part Two

The Greek word for spiritual gift is *charisma*, which comes from *charis* that means "grace."
Write your own definition of a spiritual gift:

Dr. Wagner's definition is:

"A spiritual gift is a special attribute given by the Holy Spirit to every member of
the Body of Christ, according to God's grace, for use within the context of the Body."

1. Underline what you agree with in this definition.
2. Cross out what you disagree with in this definition.

Part Three

At times, discovering and using spiritual gifts can be counterproductive. According to
Dr. Wagner, these pitfalls need to be avoided:

A. Confusion—Teaching Christians to discover spiritual gifts they received at conversion
has, in fact, caused many people—even mature believers—to become confused.

B. Rationalization—Some people tend to fix their attentions on a supposed gift and use it
as a rationalization for not fulfilling other biblical responsibilities. For example, some
might say they have the gift of pastoring, but not teaching. Or others might say they do
not have the gift of evangelism because they feel uncomfortable sharing Christ.

C. Self-deception—Some people think they have a spiritual gift when they really don't.

What can the Body of Christ do to avoid these pitfalls? Give a brief answer.

List three benefits received from spiritual gifts.

WHAT ARE THE GIFTS?

SESSION KEYS

Key Verse

"There are different kinds of gifts, but the same Spirit." 1 Corinthians 12:4

Key Idea

Every Christian and church has spiritual gifts that produce effective ministry. The Bible is clear that God wants every Christian to have and use a spiritual gift or gifts, His lost sheep to be found, and the Body of Christ to grow.

Key Resources

* Chapter 3 of the book *Your Spiritual Gifts Can Help Your Church Grow*
* Copies of the Session 3 handout, "Spiritual Gifts Cards"

Preparation

* Use Session 3 handout, "Spiritual Gifts Cards," to cut out a set of spiritual gifts cards for each group of four people. Thoroughly shuffle each set of cards. Put a large paper clip or rubber band around each set to keep them together. Also, make enough copies of the handout to pass out to every group member so that they will have a master list of gifts to refer to later in the session.
* Have extra pencils, paper and Bibles for group members.
* If you choose to do the Getting into the Word Option, be certain to invite your pastor, elder or church leader well in advance of this session.

Session 3 at a Glance

SECTION	60-MINUTE SESSION	90-MINUTE SESSION	ACTIVITY
GETTING STARTED	**5 MINUTES**	**15 MINUTES**	
Choice 1 *or*	5 Minutes	5 Minutes	Sharing Last Week *or*
Choice 2			Getting to Know You
Option		10 Minutes	Meeting More People
GETTING INTO THE WORD	**50 MINUTES**	**70 MINUTES**	
Step 1	25 Minutes	25 Minutes	Sorting Out the Gifts
Step 2	25 Minutes	25 Minutes	Two Important Gift Concepts
Option		20 Minutes	Your Church's Gift Ministry
GETTING PERSONAL	**5 MINUTES**	**5 MINUTES**	
	5 Minutes	5 Minutes	Thanking God for His Gifts

SESSION PLAN

Leader's Choice

60- and 90-minute meeting options: This session is designed to be completed in one 60-minute meeting. If you want to extend the session to a 90-minute meeting, refer to the boxes marked with the clock symbol. These options will provide additional learning experiences expanding the session to 90 minutes.

Getting Started (5 Minutes)

Choice 1—Sharing Last Week

As group members arrive, ask persons to sit in groups of four with people they did not sit with at the last session. As soon as they are seated within small groups of four, invite them to share:

* **One way the Lord really blessed me last week was:**
* **One new thing I have learned so far about spiritual gifts is:**
* **In order to get to the group today, I had to:**

Choice 2—Getting to Know You

As group members arrive, ask each of them to find one other person that he or she does not know well or has not talked with in the past week. Invite them to sit in pairs with their partners and to share:

* **Five things about my childhood you probably don't know are:**
* **Five things that have happened to me since I was 18 years old that you may not know are:**
* **One thing about spiritual gifts that really interests me is:**

Getting Started Option (10 Minutes)
Meeting More People

This option will add 10 minutes to either one of the Getting Started choices.

Ask the pairs from Choice 2 to get into groups of four people each. Have each person introduce his or her partner to the other pair using about one minute to share the new things that he or she has learned about that person. Then have each small group of four find another small group of four and go around the circle with each person introducing his or her partner.

Getting into the Word (50 Minutes)

Step 1—Sorting Out the Gifts (25 Minutes)

Now ask everyone to stay or get in a group of four people. Give one person in each group a set of spiritual gifts cards from "Spiritual Gifts Cards," which have been thoroughly mixed and shuffled. You need to refer to pages 53-54 in *Your Spiritual Gifts Can Help Your Church Grow* in order to see the listing of these gifts in the three passages: Romans 12; 1 Corinthians 12 and Ephesians 4. Ask each group of four people to sort their cards according to these three passages. Each group will have three sets of cards when they are finished sorting. Instruct them that if one gift appears in more than one passage, they should put that gift in the passage in which it first appears. Give the small groups about 10 minutes to sort their sets of gifts into the three passages. After the small groups have sorted out the gifts according to passage, let them share with the total group which gifts are found in each passage. List the gifts on a chalkboard or overhead under the heading of each passage: Romans 12; 1 Corinthians 12; Ephesians 4.

Share with the total group how Peter Wagner lists the gifts. Then in the small groups of four, share:
* **Which gifts are least familiar to you? Most familiar?**
* **Which gifts are most used in your church? Least used?**

Step 2—Two Important Gift Concepts (25 Minutes)

Dr. Wagner lists seven other gifts that are not included in these primary passages. Write this list on the board. **They are: celibacy (continence), voluntary poverty, martyrdom, hospitality, missionary, intercession and deliverance. We are going to learn about them in later sessions.**

Dr. Wagner mentions two important concepts that we need to discuss. The first is "an open-ended approach" to gifts. These seven gifts I just listed are not in the primary gift passages in the Bible. Some are found elsewhere in Scripture and all are experienced in many churches today. Dr. Wagner concedes there may be more gifts like the gift of music. In your small groups discuss:
* **Do you agree with this "open-ended approach to gifts"? Explain why or why not.**
* **Are there other gifts of the Holy Spirit that Dr. Wagner doesn't mention that you believe exist? What would they be?**

After about five minutes of sharing, bring everyone back to the total group and invite

the foursomes to share what they discussed. List on the board any other gifts they felt needed to be on the list. Discuss why they would add those gifts.

Give everyone a copy of the Session 3 handout, "Spiritual Gift Cards."

The second concept that Dr. Wagner raises is that of a "church's gift-mix." He presents the idea that every church has particular gifts that they operate in and that they may exclude or omit other gifts. Some churches and denominations may even forbid certain gifts saying that they were only for the Early Church and have since passed away. What is our church's gift-mix? Go back to your group of four and take this list of gifts from our primary Scripture passages. In the empty box on your handout, add these seven other gifts that I have listed on the board from Dr. Wagner's book. As a group, come to a consensus on the gift-mix you believe presently exists in our church. Circle those gifts that operate in our church. Put a question mark by those that might operate in the future but are not present now. Draw a line through those gifts you believe might be intentionally excluded from our church.

After about 10 minutes of sharing in small groups, gather the total group together. Discuss which gifts are operating in your church and those that might operate in the future. Find out what gifts the small group may have crossed out. Discuss why these gifts have not been allowed in your church in the past. If your church does exclude certain gifts, it would be very helpful to invite your pastor into your study and work through the following option with him or her.

Getting into the Word Option (20 Minutes)
Your Church's Gift Ministry

This option will add 20 minutes to the Getting into the Word section.

Gather the lists of spiritual gifts that you made from your gift cards at the beginning of this session. Review your list of 27 spiritual gifts. Understand that some churches and Christian leaders believe that the "sign gifts" ceased from the Body of Christ's ministry after the death of the apostles. What does your church teach or believe? You may want to invite a pastor or an elder or church leader to come and share at this point in your study. Or you may want to summarize Dr. Wagner's presentation on pages 73-77. Allow the group to discuss this freely but not to attack or degrade any particular persons. Keep focused on the biblical issue of gifts and their purpose to help a church grow and minister. Remember that the work of the Holy Spirit in gifting persons for ministry brings unity, not division. As a group with your pastor, an elder or church leader look over the lists of spiritual gifts that you have and share which gifts you believe are at work in your church. Spend time in prayer praising the Lord for gifting your church with these gifts.

Getting Personal (5 Minutes)
Thanking God for His Gifts

As a total group, spend a few minutes in silent prayer thanking the Lord for specific gifted persons who have ministered to you in the past few weeks, the gifts that the Holy Spirit is manifesting in your church and the gifts that the Holy Spirit may demonstrate in your church.

Now gather the group in a circle. Invite them to pray in unison after you: **Lord Jesus, send Your Holy Spirit to fill and use us with Your gifts that we may minister and serve one another and reach those who need You as Lord and Savior. Amen.**

Spiritual Gifts Cards

Instructions: Below are the lists of spiritual gifts from three primary passages in the New Testament. Cut out the 20 cards and thoroughly shuffle them. Give a set of 20 cards to each small group of four that you will have in your group. For example, if you have 16 group members, make up four sets of gift cards.

Note that the words in parentheses are variant translations found in several English versions of the Bible.

PROPHECY (preaching, inspired utterance)	**SERVICE** (ministry)	**TEACHING**
EXHORTATION (stimulating faith, encouraging)	**GIVING** (sharing, contributing, generosity)	**LEADERSHIP** (ruling, administration, authority)
MERCY (sympathy, comfort to the sorrowing, showing kindness)	**WISDOM** (wise advice, wise speech)	**KNOWLEDGE** (speaking with knowledge, studying)
FAITH	**HEALING**	**HELPS**
MIRACLES (doing great deeds)	**DISCERNING OF SPIRITS** (discrimination in spiritual matters)	**TONGUES** (speaking in languages never learned, ecstatic utterance)
INTERPRETATION OF TONGUES	**APOSTLE**	**EVANGELIST**
ADMINISTRATION (governments, getting others to work together)	**PASTOR** (caring for God's people)	

THE OTHER GIFTS

SESSION KEYS

Key Verse
"Each man has his own gift from God; one has this gift, another has that." 1 Corinthians 7:7

Key Idea
There are other spiritual gifts not specifically mentioned in 1 Corinthians, Romans, Ephesians and 1 Peter, which include celibacy, martyrdom, intercession, missionary and hospitality.

Key Resources
✳ Chapter 3 of the book *Your Spiritual Gifts Can Help Your Church Grow*
✳ Copies of the Session 4 handout, "The Other Gifts"
✳ Optional: *Foxe's Book of Martyrs* by John Foxe (Baker Books, 1978)

Preparation
✳ Have Bibles, blank paper and pencils and pens for all group members who may need them.
✳ If you select Choice 2 under Getting Started, have a 3x5-inch or 4x6-inch card (depending on the size of your group) for each group member.

SECTION	60-MINUTE SESSION	90-MINUTE SESSION	ACTIVITY
GETTING STARTED	**10 MINUTES**	**20 MINUTES**	
Choice 1 *or*	10 Minutes	10 Minutes	Single or Married? *or*
Choice 2			Pray for One Another
Option		10 Minutes	Think About the Gifts
GETTING INTO THE WORD	**45 MINUTES**	**65 MINUTES**	
Step 1	25 Minutes	25 Minutes	The Other Gifts
Step 2	20 Minutes	20 Minutes	Could You Be the One?
Option		20 Minutes	Sharing About Saints
GETTING PERSONAL	**5 MINUTES**	**5 MINUTES**	
	5 Minutes	5 Minutes	Thank You for Saints

S E S S I O N   P L A N

Leader's Choice

60- and 90-minute meeting options: This session is designed to be completed in one 60-minute meeting. If you want to extend the session to a 90-minute meeting, refer to the boxes marked with the clock symbol. These options will provide additional learning experiences expanding the session to 90 minutes.

Getting Started (10 Minutes)

Choice 1—Single or Married?

Warmly welcome everyone as the group arrives. Divide the group into small groups of three or four people each. Be certain that each small group has paper and pencils. Do not let spouses be in the same group. In these small groups, ask people to share: **All of us, at one time in our lives, are single. Some of us also spend part of our lives married. There are positives and negatives to both. Let's just focus on the positives today. In your small group, come up with and write down five benefits of being single and five benefits of being married.**

Give each small group about five minutes to come up with their lists and then bring everyone back to share their lists with the total group. Have fun with this.

Choice 2—Pray for One Another

As group members arrive, warmly welcome them and hand each person a 3x5-inch card

(or a 4x6-inch card for a larger group) and a pencil. Ask them to visit with every other person in the room. They are to write each person's name on their cards and two things by that person's name:

✳ One thing that person is thankful for:
✳ One prayer request that person has:

After each person has filled his or her card with everyone's prayer requests, each member is to put that card in his or her Bible and pray for those group members during the coming week.

Getting Started Option (10 Minutes)

Think About the Gifts

This option will add 10 minutes to either one of the Getting Started choices.

Ask each person in the group to list every group member's name on a piece of paper. Tell the group, **By each name, put one or more spiritual gifts that you have observed in that person's life. If you do not know a person well, simply put a question mark by his or her name indicating you need to get to know him or her better during the course of this study. After making your list, quietly pray over the list and thank the Lord for the spiritual gifts that are present in the room.**

Getting into the Word (45 Minutes)

Step 1—The Other Gifts (25 Minutes)

Peter Wagner lists five other gifts not included in these primary passages. They are: celibacy (continence), voluntary poverty, martyrdom, hospitality and missionary. We are going to learn about three of them right now and discuss missionary and voluntary poverty later.

Give everyone a copy of the Session 4 handout, "The Other Gifts." Ask everyone to fill out his or her handout. When all have completed it, ask them to share in groups of four what they have discovered. If time permits, share a story from Dr. Wagner's book or *Foxe's Book of Martyrs* about a Christian who died for his or her faith in Jesus Christ.

Now, Dr. Wagner also mentions two other gifts that some have in their lists of spiritual gifts. They are intercession and deliverance (exorcism). This completes his list of 27 spiritual gifts. Since deliverance is closely related to the gift of discernment, we will study it later. But now, we shall take a few moments to explore the gift of intercession. List on the board or overhead the following characteristics of intercessors.

Intercessors:
✳ pray longer than most;
✳ pray with more intensity;
✳ enjoy prayer more and get great personal satisfaction from praying;
✳ see more frequent and dramatic answers to their prayers;
✳ hear from God more regularly and more accurately.

As a group discuss:
✳ **What other characteristics would you add?**
✳ **Who are the powerful intercessors in our church?**
✳ **Dr. Wagner contends that 5 percent of a church do about 80 percent of the most effective praying and that 8 out of 10 intercessors are women. Do you agree or disagree? Why?**

Step 2—Could You Be the One? (20 Minutes)

Could you be celibate, a martyr or an intercessor if the Lord called and gifted you to be one? Read 1 Corinthians 7:7,8 to the group. Discuss as a total group:

✳ **Why would Paul encourage people to stay celibate? (See 1 Corinthians 7:32-34.)**

✳ **What advantages does celibacy hold for a pastor or missionary? What disadvantages?**

✳ **Some churches require their clergy or priests to be celibate. What are your beliefs about requiring this?**

Could you be a martyr? For whom or what would you die? Put this list up on a chalkboard or an overhead:

✳ Close family member; ✳ Relative; ✳ Friend; ✳ Enemy; ✳ Nation;

✳ Famous person; ✳ Child; ✳ Stranger; ✳ Acquaintance.

Find a partner. Share with that partner for whom on this list you would be willing to die, if it meant he, she or they would then know Jesus. Then share why you would or would not be willing to die for each person or thing on the list. After five minutes of sharing bring the whole group back together. Read Hebrews 11:32-40 to the group. Discuss:

✳ **What were these early Christians willing to die for?**

✳ **Is martyrdom a spiritual gift or not? Why or why not?**

✳ **Who are other martyrs through the centuries that have died for the faith to whom we owe much as Christians?** Tyndale, Hus, Joan of Arc, Peter, Justin Martyr, etc.

Could you be an intercessor? Intercessors spend hours upon hours in prayer before the Lord. They willingly give up much in life to pray for others and stand in the gap for them. Read Romans 8:26,27 and Ephesians 6:18. With your partner share:

✳ **How the Holy Spirit prays through me;**

✳ **What the Spirit prompts me to pray about;**

✳ **What are "all prayers," "all occasions" and "all the saints" referring to.**

Getting into the Word Option (20 Minutes)

Sharing About Saints

This option will add 20 minutes to the Getting into the Word section.

Share with the group more stories about martyrs from *Foxe's Book of Martyrs*. Invite people to share about how persons with the gifts of intercession or celibacy have blessed their lives. Spend time in prayer giving God thanks for these people with these gifts.

Getting Personal (5 Minutes)

Thank You for Saints

Form a closing circle. Invite each group member to share the name of one intercessor, celibate person or martyr for whom they are thankful and a brief statement of why. Go around the circle with sentence prayers for these saints, praying, **"Lord, we give thanks for...."**

The Other Gifts

The Gift of Celibacy

1. What does Paul say about celibacy in 1 Corinthians 7:7?

2. Skim over 1 Corinthians 7. What are some of the advantages of celibacy? What would some of the disadvantages of this gift be?

3. Read the following definition that Dr. Wagner gives for celibacy. How would you rewrite it in your own words to describe it to another Christian?

"The gift of celibacy is the special ability that God gives to some members of the Body of Christ to remain single and enjoy it; to be unmarried and not suffer undue sexual temptations."

Your definition:

The Gift of Martyrdom

1. What do Acts 6:12-15; 7:54-60 and 1 Corinthians 12:3 say about martyrdom?

2. Name some martyrs throughout history that you know of who had this special gift.

3. Read the following definition that Dr. Wagner gives for the gift of martyrdom. Then write a definition in your own words.

"The gift of martyrdom is a special ability that God has given to certain members of the Body of Christ to undergo suffering for the faith even to death while consistently displaying a joyous and victorious attitude that brings glory to God."

Your definition:

The Gift of Hospitality

1. What does 1 Peter 4:9,10 say about hospitality?

2. Name some people you know who have this gift.

3. Read the following definition of this gift and then write one in your own words.

"The gift of hospitality is the special ability that God gives to certain members of the Body of Christ to provide an open house and warm welcome for those in need of food and lodging."

Your definition:

FOUR THINGS GIFTS ARE NOT

S E S S I O N   K E Y S

Key Verses

"If it is contributing to the needs of others, let him give generously." Romans 12:8
"To another [is given] distinguishing between spirits." 1 Corinthians 12:10

Key Idea

We can distinguish between gifts, fruit of the Spirit and roles. There is a difference between genuine and counterfeit gifts. The gifts of giving, discerning spirits and deliverance will be explored.

Key Resources

✳ Chapter 4 of the book *Your Spiritual Gifts Can Help Your Church Grow*
✳ Copies of the Session 5 handouts, "This Is Me" and "Deliverance from the Demonic"

Preparation

✳ Have blank paper and pencils and pens for all group members.
✳ If you select Choice 2 under Getting Started, label three sheets of poster board or newsprint with one of the following titles: Fruit, Gifts, Roles. Tape each sheet on the walls around the room. Have a supply of felt-tip pens for writing on these sheets.

Session 5 at a Glance

SECTION	60-MINUTE SESSION	90-MINUTE SESSION	ACTIVITY
GETTING STARTED	**10 MINUTES**	**20 MINUTES**	
Choice 1 *or*	10 Minutes	10 Minutes	Different Views of Me *or*
Choice 2			Roles, Gifts and Fruit
Option		10 Minutes	What's the Difference?
GETTING INTO THE WORD	**45 MINUTES**	**65 MINUTES**	
Step 1	20 Minutes	20 Minutes	The Gifts of Giving and Voluntary Poverty
Step 2	25 Minutes	25 Minutes	Discerning the Spirits
Option		20 Minutes	Deliverance
GETTING PERSONAL	**5 MINUTES**	**5 MINUTES**	
	5 Minutes	5 Minutes	Individual Prayer

SESSION PLAN

Leader's Choice

60- and 90-minute meeting options: This session is designed to be completed in one 60-minute meeting. If you want to extend the session to a 90-minute meeting, refer to the boxes marked with the clock symbol. These options will provide additional learning experiences expanding the session to 90 minutes.

Getting Started (10 Minutes)

Choice 1—Different Views of Me

As everyone arrives, welcome each person and give each a copy of the Session 5 handout "This is Me," and a pen or pencil if he or she needs one.

Under the heading of Personality, write a paragraph that describes your personality. You might be outgoing, friendly, a detail person, a morning person and the like. Write this paragraph without describing your physical characteristics or your biographical background. Under the heading of Talents, write a paragraph about some of the gifts, talents and skills you have, such as cooking,

playing tennis, communicating well with others, etc. Again avoid giving any physical or biographical characteristics.

After everyone has completed his or her descriptions, proceed to collect all the sheets and shuffle them thoroughly. Now read both descriptions of various group members. After reading each one, see if the group can guess who the paragraphs describe. Take about five minutes to do this and then explain: **As you could see from working on your own paragraph descriptions and from hearing others', there is a distinct difference between personality qualities and personal skills and talents. Similarly, there are distinct spiritual differences between gifts and fruits of the Spirit, as well as the roles we have as Christians. Let's explore these together.**

Choice 2—Roles, Gifts and Fruit

As people arrive, welcome them and point them to the pieces of newsprint that you have hung on the wall. On three different pieces of newsprint or poster board titled "Gifts," "Fruit" and "Roles," ask everyone to take a felt-tip pen and list one thing on each piece of newsprint that they would think is given by the Spirit of God. For example, a gift might be teaching. A fruit might be kindness. And a role might be father, mother, elder or deacon. They may list the same thing as someone else if they wish. Then discuss:

✳ **What are the differences among these three categories? What are the similarities?**

Getting Started Option (10 Minutes)

What's the Difference?

This option will add 10 minutes to either one of the Getting Started choices.

Divide the group into three small groups. Give each small group this task: **Reflect on what the differences are among three empowered workings of the Holy Spirit in the New Testament. The Holy Spirit empowers gifts, fruit and roles in the Christian life. In each group, define what each is and how it differs from the other two. Write down a summary for each working. In five minutes, we'll all report back to each other and then discuss.**

After five minutes, have one person from each group report. Write the definitions on the chalkboard or overhead. From pages 81-87 of the book *Your Spiritual Gifts Can Help Your Church Grow*, give explanations of the workings. Then discuss:

✳ **When does the Body of Christ need to use gifts?**

✳ **How do roles minister within the Body of Christ?**

✳ **Does every Christian have some of the fruit of the Spirit or all of the fruit in differing degrees? Explain.**

Getting into the Word (45 Minutes)

Step 1—The Gifts of Giving and Voluntary Poverty (20 Minutes)

Tell the groups the stories of R. G. LeTourneau, Stanley Tam and James McCormick from pages 89-90 in *Your Spiritual Gifts Can Help Your Church Grow*. Read Leviticus 27:30 and Malachi 3:8-11 to the group. Discuss:

✳ **Why do you or don't you believe a tithe is required by God of Christians?**

✳ **Read Galatians 6:7. What consequences will a Christian experience if he or she does not tithe? What blessings are received from tithing?**

✷ **What is the difference between tithing and the kind of giving that LeTourneau, Tam and McCormick represent?**

✷ **How would they represent the spiritual gift of giving?**

✷ **What is the difference between the spiritual gift of giving and tithing?**

Ask for individuals in the group to volunteer brief testimonies of times God blessed their lives when they tithed and gave cheerfully to the Lord. Invite them to share any stories they may have of individuals they have met over the years who had the gift of giving. Read the following definition: **"The gift of giving is the special ability God gives to certain members of the Body of Christ to contribute their material resources to the work of the Lord with liberality and cheerfulness."**

✷ **How would you add to or revise this definition based on your understanding of the Scripture?**

Briefly share the stories of John Wesley and George Muller from pages 91-93 in the book. Read 1 Corinthians 13:3 to the group and the following definition of the gift of voluntary poverty: **"The gift of voluntary poverty is the special ability that God gives to certain members of the Body of Christ to renounce material comfort and luxury and adopt a personal lifestyle equivalent to those living at the poverty level in a given society in order to serve God more effectively."**

✷ **Who are some people you know who have this gift?** Twentieth-century people might include Mother Teresa and Albert Schweitzer. People in the Bible who may have had this gift were the disciples, the widow who gave out of her poverty, Paul, Barnabas, etc.

✷ **Why would it be so hard for us to receive such a gift from the Holy Spirit?** Ask everyone to pair with a partner. Give each person one minute to share all those things that it would be difficult to live without—like a car, house, refrigerator, telephone, etc.

✷ **What would be the most difficult thing to give up if Christ called you to voluntary poverty?**

The gift of giving and voluntary poverty are spiritual gifts. All are called upon to give to the Lord. But only some have the gift to give extraordinarily to the kingdom of God.

Step 2—Discerning the Spirits (25 Minutes)

Read Matthew 7:22,23; 24:24 to the group. Then discuss as a total group:

✷ **Can Satan counterfeit any spiritual gift? Which gifts are more likely to be abused in the Body of Christ?**

✷ **Share any cautions you have learned as a Christian in the use and abuse of spiritual gifts.**

✷ **How does God help us discern between genuine and counterfeit gifts?**

Share with the group the story about Raphael Gasson from pages 94-95 in the book.

Read 1 John 4:1 together as a group. Divide the total group up into three small groups. Assign one of the first three Gospels to each of the small groups. Say: **Each group has been assigned a Gospel. Appoint a recorder or secretary for each small group. Now divide up the Gospel among the rest of the small-group members so that everyone has an equal number of chapters to skim. For example, Mark has 16 chapters. If there are four of you who can skim through Mark, then have each person take four chapters. When I say "Start," take about 10 minutes as a group to skim through the chapters and find every reference to deliverance from demons and spirits. Report the references to your recorder who will write down each passage reference and a brief description of what happened. After 10 minutes, we'll discuss what we have found as a total group. Start.**

After 10 minutes, have each group report its findings while you list these passages on the board or overhead and then discuss:

✳ How many times did Jesus encounter demons and spirits? What did He do? What did the disciples do?

✳ Do we have the authority to discern spirits and deliver persons from demonic oppression?

Read the definitions from the book for the gift of discerning spirits and the gift of deliverance. **"The gift of discerning of spirits is the special ability that God gives to some members of the Body of Christ to know with assurance whether certain behavior purported to be of God is in reality divine, human or satanic. The gift of deliverance is the special ability that God gives to certain members of the Body of Christ to cast out demons and evil spirits."**

✳ **How would you define and describe these gifts differently than Dr. Peter Wagner?**

✳ **Relate an experience you have had in using or witnessing the use of these gifts.**

Getting into the Word Option (20 Minutes)

Deliverance

This option will add 20 minutes to the Getting into the Word section.

Give everyone a copy of the Session 5 handout "Deliverance from the Demonic." Ask each person to complete the handout and then discuss:

✳ **How can the Body of Christ resist the influence or oppression of these demonic attacks?**

✳ **When someone has been involved in one of these demonic activities, how would you approach him or her about stopping or being delivered?**

Getting Personal (5 Minutes)

Individual Prayer

Ask each person to share an area for prayer that he or she felt a personal need for in this session. Some may wish to pray for more fruit in their Christian walks. Others may desire to pray for the one of the gifts that you studied today. Others may wish to pray for friends or family members involved in evil spiritual activities from which they need to be set free.

If you have a group of more than 10 people, invite people to pray for one another in pairs.

If you have a small group, have people share their prayer requests and then have an open time of prayer with the leader closing the prayer time by praying something like this: **Lord Jesus, grant each request through the power of Your Holy Spirit. Deliver from bondage each person mentioned through the blood of Jesus Christ. Amen.**

This Is Me

Personality

_____
_____
_____
_____
_____
_____
_____
_____

Talents

_____
_____
_____
_____
_____
_____
_____
_____
_____

Deliverance from the Demonic

1. Below is a list of some demonic activities. If you have ever participated in one, circle it. If you know someone who is active in one of these, put a check by it.

_____ Séance   _____ Ouija boards   _____ Fortune tellers

_____ Astrology   _____ Witchcraft   _____ Satanism

_____ Psychics   _____ New Age   _____ Secret societies

_____ Tarot cards   _____ White or black magic   _____ Metaphysics

_____ Cults   _____ Trances   _____ Praying to the
                                                                     spirits of the dead

2. Read Matthew 12:25-37. Make a list of the ways you know that a given activity is demonic.

3. Read 1 John 4:1-3. How does one discern evil spirits?

4. Are you able to discern evil spirits from the Spirit of God? Who do you know who can discern spirits? Who do you know that can pray for those demonized to be delivered?

5. Write a prayer to cover and protect yourself, your family and your church from demonic attack.

SESSION 6

DISCOVERING SPIRITUAL GIFTS

SESSION KEYS

Key Verse

"Now about spiritual gifts, brothers, I do not want you to be ignorant." 1 Corinthians 12:1

Key Idea

Discover how to find your spiritual gifts and learn about the gift of teaching.

Key Resources

* Chapter 5 of the book Your Spiritual Gifts Can Help Your Church Grow
* Copies of the Session 6 handouts, "Which Gifts Are for Me?" and "Steps for Discovering Your Spiritual Gifts"

Preparation

* Have Bibles, blank paper and pencils and pens for all group members who may need them.

SECTION	60-MINUTE SESSION	90-MINUTE SESSION	ACTIVITY
GETTING STARTED	**10 MINUTES**	**20 MINUTES**	
Choice 1 *or*	10 Minutes	10 Minutes	Before You Discover Your Spiritual Gifts *or* Which Gifts Are for Me?
Choice 2			
Option		10 Minutes	Gifts in the Church
GETTING INTO THE WORD	**45 MINUTES**	**65 MINUTES**	
Step 1	25 Minutes	25 Minutes	What You Need to Receive Gifts
Step 2	20 Minutes	20 Minutes	The Gift of Teaching
Option		20 Minutes	Praying for Teachers
GETTING PERSONAL	**5 MINUTES**	**5 MINUTES**	
	5 Minutes	5 Minutes	Thank God for Teachers

S E S S I O N   P L A N

Leader's Choice

60- and 90-minute meeting options: This session is designed to be completed in one 60-minute meeting. If you want to extend the session to a 90-minute meeting, refer to the boxes marked with the clock symbol. These options will provide additional learning experiences expanding the session to 90 minutes.

Getting Started (10 Minutes)

Choice 1—Before You Discover Your Spiritual Gifts

As group members arrive, welcome them and ask them to greet everyone in the class by saying: **One spiritual gift I may have is (gift). What about you?**

As a group discuss:

* **How would a person discover if he or she really had a certain spiritual gift?**
* **If a person thought that he or she might have a certain spiritual gift, how could that be confirmed?**

List all of the group's ideas on the chalkboard or overhead.

Choice 2—Which Gifts Are for Me?

Give everyone a copy of the Session 6 handout "Which Gifts Are for Me?"

After everyone has completed the handout, have each person go to three other people in the group and share with them the gift he or she sees in each person's life and then discuss:

✳ **How do we identify a gift in our lives or someone else's?**

....

Getting Started Option (10 Minutes)

Gifts in the Church

This option will add 10 minutes to either one of the Getting Started choices.

Give everyone a copy of the Session 6 handout "Which Gifts Are for Me?" if they do not already have it. If you have not used it already, ask everyone to complete the instructions at home. However, use the list of spiritual gifts to discuss:

✳ **Which gifts are most needed in our church?**

✳ **How could we discover those gifts?**

✳ **Which gifts are most evident in our church? How could we minister those gifts more effectively?**

....

Getting into the Word (45 Minutes)

Step 1—What You Need to Receive Gifts (25 Minutes)

Write these verses on the chalkboard or overhead: Acts 2:38; Romans 10:9; 1 Corinthians 12:1; 1 Timothy 4:14; and James 1:5.

Have everyone in the group look up and then discuss these passages.

Peter Wagner states that there are four fundamental prerequisites toward finding our spiritual gifts. Each set of Scriptures gives us an indication of what these might be. What four prerequisites do you think these Scriptures indicate? Allow the group to discuss each one and then list their ideas on the board or overhead. After the group's discussion, list Dr. Wagner's suggestions on the board:

1. You must be a Christian.

2. You must believe in spiritual gifts.

3. You have to be willing to work—to use your gift(s).

4. You have to pray.

Discuss if the group would add to or revise this list in any way.

Give each group member a copy of the Session 6 handout "Steps for Discovering Your Spiritual Gifts."

Dr. Wagner suggests five steps for finding your spiritual gift(s). Look at your handout. Indicate which steps you have taken and where you are right now in laying hold of your spiritual gifts.

Give everyone about three to four minutes to fill out the survey then put people into pairs and tell them to:

✳ **Share one step that you have taken.**

✳ **Share one step that you would be willing to take.**

✳ **Share one step that you are still reluctant to take.**

Step 2—The Gift of Teaching (20 Minutes)

Ask the group to brainstorm all the skills it takes to teach children, youth and adults effectively.

✳ How is the spiritual gift of teaching different from the natural ability to teach?

Read the definition of this gift to the group. "The gift of teaching is the special ability that God gives to certain members of the Body of Christ to communicate information relevant to the health and ministry of the Body and its members in such a way that others will learn."

Ask the group to add to or revise this definition.

Ask for two or three group members to give testimonies about Christian teachers they may have had that made a significant impact on them spiritually. Then as a group have a prayer of corporate thanksgiving for those who have the gift of teaching. Have each person speak the first name of a Christian teacher that he or she is thankful for and then the whole group will pray in unison: **Thank You Lord for the Christian teacher, (name).**

Getting into the Word Option (20 Minutes)

Praying for Teachers

This option will add 20 minutes to the Getting into the Word section.

Ask each group member to take a piece of paper and list every teacher in your church that he or she can remember by name. Take time to pray for each teacher and ask God's anointing and protection to be upon them.

Now list every teacher who teaches at your church. Put that list on the board in front of the group. Spend time giving thanks and praying for these teachers.

Put the leader or teacher of this study in the middle of the group. Have the group gather around and lay hands on this teacher or join hands around this teacher. Pray for God's anointing on the teacher of this study.

Getting Personal (5 Minutes)

Thank God for Teachers

Ask each group member to write down the names of two or three teachers from your church that he or she is willing to pray for in the coming week. Spend time in silent prayer as a group and then ask the group to pray in unison after you: **Heavenly Father, we thank You for teachers. May we continue to support those with the gift of teaching through learning and prayer. In Jesus' name. Amen.**

Which Gifts Are for Me?

Circle the gifts that you believe you may have. Put a question mark by the ones you desire to know more about.

_____ Prophecy	_____ Service	_____ Teaching
_____ Exhortation	_____ Giving	_____ Leadership
_____ Mercy	_____ Wisdom	_____ Knowledge
_____ Faith	_____ Healing	_____ Miracles
_____ Discerning of spirits	_____ Tongues	_____ Apostle
_____ Pastor	_____ Helps	_____ Interpretation of tongues
_____ Administration	_____ Evangelist	_____ Celibacy
_____ Voluntary poverty	_____ Martyrdom	_____ Hospitality
_____ Missionary	_____ Intercession	_____ Deliverance

Look around your group. Put initials by the gifts of the people in the group who have those gifts. Don't guess. Just do the ones you feel most certain in identifying.

Steps for Discovering Your Spiritual Gifts

If you have taken this step, write **Yes** before the step.
If you have not taken a particular step but are willing Ito try that step,
write a **+** before the statement.
If you have not taken a step and are unwilling at this time to try it,
write a **–** by that step. (These steps are not in a particular progression or order.)

_____ **1.** Explore the possibilities.

—— Study the Bible.

—— Learn my church's position on gifts.

—— Read extensively about spiritual gifts.

—— Get to know gifted people.

—— Make gifts a conversation piece.

_____ **2.** Experiment with as many gifts as you can.

—— Look for needs that God can meet through you.

—— Use a gifts inventory.

_____ **3.** Examine your feelings. Is the gift you are using giving you excitement or a feeling that this is what you want to do more than anything else?

_____ **4.** Evaluate your effectiveness.

_____ **5.** Expect confirmation from other Christians.

THE PASTOR'S GIFT-MIX

S E S S I O N   K E Y S

Key Verses

"It was he who gave some to be apostles, some to be prophets, some to be evangelists, and some to be pastors and teachers, to prepare God's people for works of service, so that the body of Christ may be built up."
Ephesians 4:11,12
(See also: Acts 1—6)

Key Idea

The gifts of pastoring, faith, exhortation, administration and leadership are most commonly used by the Holy Spirit to lead a church and help it grow.

Key Resources

* Chapter 6 of the book *Your Spiritual Gifts Can Help Your Church Grow*
* Copies of the Session 7 handout, "Gifts for Leading a Healthy Local Church"

Preparation

* Have Bibles, blank paper and pencils and pens for all group members who may need them.

Session 7 at a Glance

SECTION	60-MINUTE SESSION	90-MINUTE SESSION	ACTIVITY
GETTING STARTED	**10 MINUTES**	**20 MINUTES**	
Choice 1 *or*	10 Minutes	10 Minutes	What's a Pastor? *or*
Choice 2			Pastors that Made a Difference
Option		10 Minutes	Leaders Make a Difference
GETTING INTO THE WORD	**45 MINUTES**	**65 MINUTES**	
Step 1	20 Minutes	20 Minutes	The Gifts of Pastor and Leaders
Step 2	25 Minutes	25 Minutes	What Gifts Help a Church?
Option		20 Minutes	Gifts in Acts
GETTING PERSONAL	**5 MINUTES**	**5 MINUTES**	
	5 Minutes	5 Minutes	Pray for Our Pastor and Leaders

S E S S I O N   P L A N

···

Leader's Choice

60- and 90-minute meeting options: This session is designed to be completed in one 60-minute meeting. If you want to extend the session to a 90-minute meeting, refer to the boxes marked with the clock symbol. These options will provide additional learning experiences expanding the session to 90 minutes.

···

Getting Started (10 Minutes)

Choice 1—What's a Pastor?

As group members arrive, welcome them and ask them to find as partners people that they do not know well. Ask them to share with one another about their families, work and one good thing that the Lord did in their lives in the past week. Give all the pairs about three minutes to do this. Then say:

* **In one or two words, discuss synonyms for the word "pastor."**
* **Next, decide on the two most important qualities you believe a pastor should have. Avoid focusing on tasks like teaching or preaching.**
  Now list from the total group on the chalkboard or overhead what words they have for "pastor" and what qualities they believe a pastor should have. Then ask:
* **Are pastors always those who are the senior ministers leading churches or could lay people be pastors? Explain.**

Choice 2—Pastors that Made a Difference

As group members arrive, welcome them and put them into groups of four people each. Ask them to share:

* **Something wonderful the Lord did in your lives during the past week.**
* **About a pastor who most influenced your spiritual lives.**

After they have had a few moments to share with one another, ask **How many of you shared about a minister? How many shared about an elder or another lay person who pastored you? Why do we define being a pastor as the senior minister of a church? Can someone have the gift of pastor without being in the ministry full-time?**

Getting Started Option (10 Minutes)

Leaders Make a Difference

This option will add 10 minutes to either one of the Getting Started choices.

To continue your group sharing say: **Pastors as well as other church leaders, such as elders, deacons, teachers and youth workers are very important in ministering to our lives. Let's go around the group and share brief stories or testimonies about how a church leader from the past really touched our lives.** Have as many share as time permits.

Getting into the Word (45 Minutes)

Step 1—The Gifts of the Pastor and Leaders (20 Minutes)

Peter Wagner cites many studies that demonstrate that the key person in a growing church is the minister. However, the senior minister of a large growing church may not have the gift of pastor. Still, there are four gifts essential for the health and vitality of the local church. The senior minister probably will have some but not all of them. But they need to be present in the leadership of a church.

Look over the list of 27 gifts and decide which 4 you believe are necessary for a healthy local church to have among its leaders. Take five to seven minutes for this, then discuss:

* **Which gifts are important for the senior minister to have? Why?**
* **If the senior minister does not have at least one of these gifts, then what should a church do?**

After the group has discussed these questions, identify the following gifts as those which are necessary for the church leadership to have if a church is to grow spiritually and stay healthy:

* Pastor
* Exhortation
* Faith
* Administration
* Leadership

Give everyone a copy of the Session 7 handout, "Gifts for Leading the Church."

Divide the group into pairs or threesomes. Ask everyone to complete their handouts individually and then share in their trios or pairs what they have written. Take about 10 minutes for this.

Step 2—What Gifts Help a Church? (25 Minutes)

The beginning and growth of the Early Church is described in the book of Acts. Turn to that book and let's explore how the gifts were exercised in the

first part of Acts. If your group has 12 or more people, divide the total group into six small groups of two or more people in a group. Assign each small group one of the first six chapters of Acts. If the group is smaller than 12 persons, assign every person one of the first six chapters of Acts. **On a piece of paper, list the five gifts of leading and helping a church grow and mature in Jesus Christ: "faith," "exhortation," "pastoring," "administration" and "leadership."**

By each gift, list any passage references in the first six chapters that would illustrate the use of that gift in the Early Church. After doing this, make an additional list with Scripture references of any other gifts you see manifested in your chapter. Take about 10 minutes to make your list.

After everyone has completed his or her list, as a total group, put this list of five gifts on the board or overhead. As a total group list all the passages that were discovered in Acts 1—6 that refer to these gifts. Then list all the other gifts group members discovered and references where they are found. Discuss:

* **How did the Holy Spirit use gifts in the Early Church to grow the Body of Christ and inspire leadership?**
* **Which manifestations of these gifts do we see in our church?**
* **After studying Acts 1—6 as a group, would you add any gifts to Dr. Wagner's list of five gifts necessary for leading and growing a church? If so, which ones and why?**

Getting into the Word Option (20 Minutes)
Gifts in Acts

This option will add 20 minutes to the Getting into the Word section.

One place in the New Testament that lists some of the leadership gifts needed in the Body of Christ is in Ephesians 4:11-16. Read this passage to the group as they follow along in their own Bibles. Discuss:

* **Which of these gifts were evident in the Early Church?**

Divide the total group into four small groups. Assign seven chapters to each small group.

Group 1: Acts 1—7   Group 2: Acts 8—14

Group 3: Acts 15—21   Group 4: Acts 22—28

Look for people in your chapters who demonstrated in their lives one of the gifts mentioned in Ephesians 4:11-16. Write down their names and something about how they used their gifts. After about 10 to 12 minutes, bring all the group members back together to share. List the people they have discovered on the board or overhead. Put the names of their gifts beside their names. Ask the group members to share briefly how these church leaders in Acts used their gifts.

Getting Personal (5 Minutes)
Pray for Our Pastor and Leaders

Have everyone look once again at the list of gifts needed for leading a healthy local church. Divide group members into pairs. Invite each partner to share one gift that your church needs in its leadership for growth to occur and one gift from this list in which the person desires growth.

Ask the partners to pray for one another, your pastor and the leadership of your church.

Gifts for Leading a Healthy Local church

Pastor

Definition: "The gift of pastor is the special ability that God gives to certain members of the Body of Christ to assume long-term personal responsibility for the spiritual welfare of a group of believers."

The people in our church's leadership who strongly demonstrate this gift are:

Administration

Definition: "The gift of administration is the special ability that God gives to some members of the Body of Christ to understand clearly the immediate and long-range goals of a particular unit of the Body of Christ and to devise and execute effective plans for the accomplishment of those goals."

The people in our church's leadership who strongly demonstrate this gift are:

Faith

Definition: "The gift of faith is the special ability that God gives to some members of the Body of Christ to discern with extraordinary confidence the will and purposes of God for the future of His work."

The people in our church's leadership who strongly demonstrate this gift are:

Leadership

Definition: "The gift of leadership is the special ability that God gives to certain members of the Body of Christ to set goals in accordance with God's purpose for the future and to communicate these goals to others in such a way that they voluntarily and harmoniously work together to accomplish those goals for the glory of God."

The people in our church's leadership who strongly demonstrate this gift are:

Exhortation

Definition: "The gift of exhortation is the special ability that God gives to certain members of the Body of Christ to minister words of comfort, consolation, encouragement and counsel to other members of the Body in such a way that they feel helped and healed."

The people in our church's leadership who strongly demonstrate this gift are:

Put, in order of strength, the gifts your minister demonstrates.

THE EVANGELIST: THE PRIMARY ORGAN FOR GROWTH

SESSION KEYS

Key Verse

"And the Lord added to their number daily those who were being saved." Acts 2:47

Key Idea

The gift of evangelist is exceedingly important for conversion growth within the Body of Christ. While everyone is to be a witness for Jesus Christ, some are gifted to be evangelists.

Key Resources

✱ Chapter 7 of the book *Your Spiritual Gifts Can Help Your Church Grow*
✱ Copies of the Session 8 handouts, "The Gift of Evangelist" and "Something Good Out of Nowhere!"

Preparation

✱ Have Bibles, blank paper and pencils and pens for all group members who may need them.
✱ If you select Getting Started Choice 2, have a 3x5-inch card for each person in the group. On one side of each card list a life-threatening disease, i.e. cancer, bubonic plague, AIDS, heart disease, diphtheria, pneumonia, etc. On the other side of each card write "The cure for all diseases."

SECTION	60-MINUTE SESSION	90-MINUTE SESSION	ACTIVITY
GETTING STARTED	**10 MINUTES**	**20 MINUTES**	
Choice 1 *or*	10 Minutes	10 Minutes	Good News *or*
Choice 2			No Good News
Option		10 Minutes	Do We Share?
GETTING INTO THE WORD	**45 MINUTES**	**65 MINUTES**	
Step 1	25 Minutes	25 Minutes	Who Can Be an Evangelist?
Step 2	20 Minutes	20 Minutes	Who Is an Evangelist?
Option		20 Minutes	On-the-Road Evangelist
GETTING PERSONAL	**5 MINUTES**	**5 MINUTES**	
	5 Minutes	5 Minutes	Evangelists' Fruit

S E S S I O N   P L A N

Leader's Choice

60- and 90-minute meeting options: This session is designed to be completed in one 60-minute meeting. If you want to extend the session to a 90-minute meeting, refer to the boxes marked with the clock symbol. These options will provide additional learning experiences expanding the session to 90 minutes.

Getting Started (10 Minutes)

Choice 1—Good News

As people arrive, tell them to think of as much good news as they can to share. This may be personal good news, good news about people they know or good news they have heard through the media. Spend about five minutes with everyone mixing thoroughly throughout the whole group telling as many people as possible their good news.

Now instruct everyone to think of at least one piece of bad news to share, and tell it to as many people as he or she can in two minutes. Discuss:
* **What's easier to share—good news or bad news? Why?**
* **Which stays in your mind longer? Why?**
* **Which was easier to think of initially? Why?**

Choice 2—No Good News

Hand one 3x5-inch card to each person as he or she arrives. **On your cards you have bad news on one side and good news on the other side. Share your bad news**

about the disease you found out you have contracted. However, do not share with anyone the good news that's on the other side of your card. Try to tell everyone in the group your bad news. **Go.** Give the group about five minutes to share its bad news. Then discuss as a total group:

* **How hard was it to share your bad news?**
* **What feelings did you have when you knew that you had good news but you could not share it?**
* **Now tell your good news to everyone you talked to.**

Getting Started Option (10 Minutes)

Do We Share?

This option will add 10 minutes to either one of the Getting Started choices.

There is so much bad news all around us. Yet, Christians have the best news in the world. Why are we reluctant to share the good news of Jesus Christ? Discuss. **Do you have to have the gift of evangelist to share the gospel?** Discuss. **Since all Christians are commanded to share the gospel and witness about Jesus, what does the gift of evangelist do for a person to empower him or her to share the gospel beyond what every Christian does?** Discuss.

Getting into the Word (45 Minutes)

Step 1—Who Can Be an Evangelist? (25 Minutes)

* **Name some persons who are gifted as evangelists.**

Put the list on the board or overhead. This list may include Billy Graham, Leighton Ford, D. L. Moody, Billy Sunday, the apostle Paul, etc.

Give everyone a copy of the Session 8 handout "The Gift of Evangelist." Ask group members to complete their handouts. Give five minutes for this.

Ask everyone to find a partner and to share how he or she has completed his or her handout. Then discuss as a total group:

* **What are the most important qualities that the Holy Spirit gives to a person with the gift of evangelist?**
* **Who are the evangelists within our midst?**
* **What should Christians who do not have this special gift do to enable and support those who do?**

Ask the pairs to turn in their Bibles to John 4:1-26. **In the story of Jesus talking to the Samaritan woman, we see a wonderful model of sharing the gospel. Read the story and then, as a pair, list all of the qualities Jesus exhibited as He shared the good news about Himself. List those qualities on the back of your handouts.** Give the pairs about five minutes to do this and then as a total group list on a chalkboard or overhead all of the qualities they discovered. Ask the group to pick two or three they feel are most important and circle those qualities. That list may include:

* Jesus spoke to a woman of a different race.
* Jesus crossed over cultural boundaries.
* Jesus challenged false religious ideas.
* Jesus spoke the truth in love.
* Jesus confronted sin realistically but not cruelly nor judgmentally.
* Jesus offered good news about something the world could not offer.
* Jesus inspired the woman to go tell others the good news.

Step 2— Who Is an Evangelist? (20 Minutes)

Peter Wagner insists that while every Christian is a witness, not every Christian is an evangelist. Witness is a Christian role. Being an evangelist is a gift of the Holy Spirit. Read the following quote to the group and then discuss: "**My role as a Christian is to be a witness for my Lord at any time, and I am delighted when God gives me the opportunity. But I have found that whenever I force it, I blow it. So I let God do it for me. When He doesn't, I stick to exercising my spiritual gift rather than my Christian role.**"

Whoever uses his or her lack of having the spiritual gift of evangelist as a cop-out from witnessing displeases God. But whoever insists that another person divert valuable energy that could be used for exercising a spiritual gift into unproductively fulfilling a Christian role likewise displeases God.

✳ **How do we force Christians into using gifts that are not theirs?**

✳ **How can we encourage Christians to witness for Jesus without putting guilt trips on them?**

Ask for three volunteers to do the reader's skit from the Session 8 handout, "Something Good Out of Nowhere!" Use men or women. If you use women simply change Phil to Phyllis and Nathan to Natanya. Have fun. After the skit, discuss:

✳ **What made Philip's witness so effective?**

✳ **Does one have to be an evangelist to witness the way Philip did?**

✳ **How would a person with the gift of evangelist witness differently to Nathaniel?**

Getting into the Word Option (20 Minutes)

On-the-Road Evangelist

This option will add 20 minutes to the Getting into the Word section.

Have everyone in the group read Acts 8:1-4,26-40. You may have someone read the passages aloud while others follow in their own Bibles. Then go to the board and list what the group shares in response to this statement:

✳ **Name every quality and empowerment from the Holy Spirit that you see at work in Philip the evangelist.**

Ask people in the group to answer the following questions:

✳ **Who accepted Jesus Christ as Lord and Savior through a person with the gift of evangelist? Share your story.**

✳ **How else do people come to conversion to Jesus Christ?**

✳ **What does a church need to do to follow up with people who are converted under an evangelist?**

✳ **What do we do in our church to nurture and spiritually mature new converts?**

✳ **How can we as the Body of Christ encourage the upcoming generation to seek the gift of evangelist?**

Getting Personal (5 Minutes)

Evangelists' Fruit

In pairs, share with one another how you were converted to Jesus Christ. Pray and thank God for everyone by name whom you can remember who played a part in your conversion. Also pray and thank God for every living evangelist you can name. Finally, ask the Lord to send His Holy Spirit to raise up evangelists for the coming generation.

The Gift of Evangelist

1. Write your definition of the gift of evangelist.

2. Check the qualities you believe the Holy Spirit gives to a person with the gift of evangelist:

- ❑ Love for others
- ❑ Zeal
- ❑ Good speaking ability
- ❑ Friendliness
- ❑ Passion

- ❑ Love for Jesus
- ❑ Compassion for the lost
- ❑ Knowledge of the Scriptures
- ❑ Extroverted personality

3. Circle two of the above qualities you believe are essential to an evangelist.

4. Read the definition of the gift of evangelist. "The gift of evangelist is the special ability that God gives to certain members of the Body of Christ to share the gospel with unbelievers in such a way that men and women become Jesus' disciples and responsible members of the Body of Christ."

Name the people you personally know who have this gift.

Something Good out of Nowhere!

Scene: Philip meets Jesus and then goes to tell Nathaniel. Nathaniel then meets Jesus. Taken from John 1:43-51.

Have Philip and Jesus walk across the front of the room from different directions and then almost run into each other.

Jesus: Hey Phil, you're going the wrong direction. Make a right turn and follow Me.

Phil: Right man. Be right back. I've got to tell Nathan about this.

Nathan: (Very relaxed, sitting down and sipping a cup of coffee or juice.) Yo, Phil, what's happenin'?

Phil: 'Than, you won't believe this. I just met the main man, the top dude, the Messiah!

Nathan: You serious?

Phil: Great, man, come see Him. (Starts pulling on Nathan to get up and come see Jesus.)

Nathan: So where is this guy from, man?

Phil: He lives in Nazareth.

Nathan: You serious?

Phil: No lie. Come and see.

Nathan: Ain't nothing ever good come out of Nazareth. I gotta' see this man. (Starts walking toward Jesus and stops suddenly.)

Jesus: Yo', bro', I know you...sitting around sipping your drink and wondering about Me.

Nathan: Whoa, Phil ain't no liar. You are my main man.

Jesus: You ain't seen nothin' yet. The best is yet to come. (All three leave the front of the room arm in arm.)

UNDERSTANDING THE MISSIONARY GIFT

S E S S I O N   K E Y S

Key Verse

"But you will receive power when the Holy Spirit comes on you; and you will be my witnesses in Jerusalem, and in all Judea and Samaria, and to the ends of the earth." Acts 1:8

Key Idea

The gift of missionary is still needed in the world today to fulfill the Great Commission of Jesus Christ.

Key Resources

✳ Chapter 8 of the book *Your Spiritual Gifts Can Help Your Church Grow*
✳ Copies of the Session 9 handout, "How Churches Grow"

Preparation

✳ Have Bibles, blank paper and pencils and pens for all group members who may need them.
✳ If you choose to do Getting Started Choice 1, have a potted plant and some seed available.
✳ If you choose to do Getting Started Choice 2, have pictures of people available.
✳ Have a world map and a list of the missionaries your church and/or denomination supports.
✳ If you chose to do the Getting into the Word Option, extend an invitation for your pastor or a missionary to join your group.

Session 9 at a Glance

SECTION	60-MINUTE SESSION	90-MINUTE SESSION	ACTIVITY
GETTING STARTED	**10 MINUTES**	**20 MINUTES**	
Choice 1 *or*	10 Minutes	10 Minutes	How Does It Grow? *or*
Choice 2			What is Growth?
Option		10 Minutes	How Churches Get Started
GETTING INTO THE WORD	**45 MINUTES**	**65 MINUTES**	
Step 1	20 Minutes	20 Minutes	Missionaries Grow Churches
Step 2	25 Minutes	25 Minutes	Are Missionaries Needed Today?
Option		20 Minutes	Bible Missionaries and Apostles
GETTING PERSONAL	**5 MINUTES**	**5 MINUTES**	
	5 Minutes	5 Minutes	Missionary Support

SESSION PLAN

Leader's Choice

60- and 90-minute meeting options: This session is designed to be completed in one 60-minute meeting. If you want to extend the session to a 90-minute meeting, refer to the boxes marked with the clock symbol. These options will provide additional learning experiences expanding the session to 90 minutes.

Getting Started (10 Minutes)

Choice 1—How Does It Grow?

Materials needed: A potted plant and some seed.

Warmly welcome people as they arrive and have them be seated. Put a potted plant in front of the group. Ask everyone to brainstorm all the different ways that a plant can grow. List all the different suggestions on a chalkboard or overhead. Some of the suggestions might be:

* A plant can grow underground by increasing its root system.
* It can grow above ground by increasing its leaves and branches.

* It can grow by bearing seed.
* It can grow by rooting new plants from cuttings.

    Discuss:
* **How are the ways that a plant grows paralleled by a church growing?**
* **What are the different ways a church can grow?**

Choice 2—What Is Growth?

Materials needed: Pictures of people.

Warmly welcome people as they arrive and have them find seats. Show the group a set of pictures of people from all different kinds of ethnic and age groupings. Ask the group to make suggestions on all the different ways that people grow. As they brainstorm, list their ideas on a chalkboard or overhead. Some of the things on that list might be:

* People grow by reproducing themselves—having children.
* People grow spiritually.
* People grow intellectually.
* People grow emotionally.
* People grow physically.

    Now ask:
* **How does human growth parallel church growth? How is it different from church growth?**

Getting Started Option (10 Minutes)

How Churches Get Started

This option will add 10 minutes to either one of the Getting Started choices.

Let's continue our discussion of growth by looking at various churches to which we have belonged. Some of you may have been in the same church all your lives, while others have been in different churches over the years. Think of one church you have been in and think about how it was started. Let's list all the ways churches we have known personally have been started.

List on the board all the different ways churches may be started. They may include:

* A church divides into two churches.
* Pioneers in an area plant the first church of that denomination.
* Missionaries or church planters go out from one church to start another.
* A denomination or group moves to a geographical area or into a new ethnic group to start a "mission" church.

    Then ask the group to discuss:
* **What do you believe is the best way to start a church in the same city? Same region? Same state? Another state? Another nation?**

Getting into the Word (45 Minutes)

Step 1—Missionaries Grow Church (20 Minutes)

There are different types of growth for the Body of Christ. Peter Wagner identifies these kinds of growth. Pass out copies of the Session 9 handout. Look at the different kinds of evangelistic growth that Dr. Wagner describes. Circle

the kind(s) of evangelism and growth our church has experienced in the past and is experiencing now.

Discuss as a group what the members circled and why.

* **What are our church's priorities for growth? Are our growth goals and objectives being realized? Why or why not?**

* **Which form of evangelism and missionary work would be the most difficult?**

Dr. Wagner's definition of the gift of missionary is "The gift of missionary is the special ability that God gives to some members of the Body of Christ to minister whatever other spiritual gifts they have in a second culture."

* **How is missionary work today done differently than it was in the first half of this century?**

Step 2—Are Missionaries Needed Today? (25 Minutes)

Invite everyone in the group to stand. **I am going to read a statement about world evangelism and missionary work. I will point to one wall as representing one answer and the other wall as representing another. Move as close to the wall as you wish representing what you believe. You may stand anywhere you wish between the two walls choosing a place that best represents your position or belief. After everyone has positioned himself or herself, I will give you the answer.**

1. **There are over 5.5 billion people in the world. Right wall is true. Left wall is false.**
   Answer: True

2. **How many active Christians are there in the world? Right wall represents more than 540 million. Left wall represents less than 430 million.**
   Answer: More than 540 million.

3. **How many people in the world are so distant from a Christian culture that it is very difficult to reach them? Right wall is less than a million. Left wall is more than two million.**
   Answer: 2.1 million.

4. **How many different people and cultural groupings do these 2.1 million people represent? Right wall is less than 1,000. Left wall is more than 6,000.**
   Answer: More than 6,000.

   Discuss:

* **Why are churches doing less and less missionary work?**

* **What are some ways these people could be reached?**

* **Do we personally know our missionaries? What is our church doing to encourage people to go into the mission field?**

Ask everyone to read Matthew 28:18-20. Divide the whole group into four groups. Assign each of the small groups one of the verbs in the Great Commission: "go," "make disciples," "baptize" and "teach."

Discuss as a group how that missionary mandate is fulfilled in your:

* church;

* community;

* groups or denominations of church;

* outreach overseas.

Getting into the Word Option (20 Minutes)

Bible Missionaries and Apostles

This option will add 20 minutes to the Getting into the Word section.

Name all the people in the Bible who were missionaries. Put their suggestions on the chalkboard. That list may include Silas, Barnabas, Paul, Thomas, Peter and Philip.

✳ **What is the difference between a missionary and an apostle?**

According to Dr. Wagner, "The gift of apostle is the special ability that God gives to certain members of the Body of Christ to assume and exercise general leadership over a number of churches with extraordinary authority in spiritual matters that is spontaneously recognized and appreciated by those churches."

✳ **Do you believe there are modern-day apostles? If so, name some.**

✳ **What are some encouraging ways that apostles can exercise their leadership? What are some abuses?**

Invite your pastor to come and share with your group about your church's missionaries and his understanding of the gift of apostle, or invite a missionary to come and share with your group about modern-day missions work.

Getting Personal (5 Minutes)

Missionary Support

Get a world map and mark every place a missionary from your church and/or denomination serves. List their names on the map as well. Have everyone in the group take a name of a missionary and begin praying for them during the next week. Close in a group circle with each person praying a brief prayer for his or her missionary.

How Churches Grow

1. In *Your Spiritual Gifts Can Help Your Church Grow*, these types of evangelistic growth are identified:

E-1   Evangelism—winning those of your own culture to Jesus Christ.

E-2   Evangelism—winning those of a slightly different cultural background than yours to Jesus Christ.

E-3   Evangelism—evangelizing those of a vastly different culture than yours to Jesus Christ.

E-O   Evangelism—winning those who are already church members to Jesus Christ.

Circle the kind(s) of evangelism most common to our church.

2. Dr. Wagner also identifies four kinds of church growth:

_____   Internal Growth—people who are already members of the Body of Christ are growing spiritually and in deeper fellowship with one another.

_____   Expansion Growth—increasing the number of church members.

_____   Extension Growth—planting new churches in a similar culture.

_____   Bridging Growth—planting new churches in different cultures.

Prioritize the kinds of growth our church focuses on from the top priority (1) to the lowest priority (4).

Read Acts 1:7-8. List the kinds of growth and evangelism that are emphasized in this passage.

THE REST OF THE BODY

SESSION KEYS

Key Verse

"Now to each one the manifestation of the Spirit is given for the common good." 1 Corinthians 12:7

Key Idea

The primary gift for the total health of the local church is pastor while the primary gift for church growth is evangelist. There are many other gifts that support and nurture these gifts.

Key Resources

* Chapter 9 of the book *Your Spiritual Gifts Can Help Your Church Grow*
* Copies of the Session 10 handout, "Gifts for the Rest of the Body"

Preparation

* Have Bibles, blank paper and pencils and pens for all group members who may need them.
* If you choose to do Getting Started Option 1, have one 3x5-inch card for each group member. Write one of these body part or organs on each card. Have an equal number of "Essential for Survival" and "Nonessential for Survival" cards. If you have more than 16 people in your group, then list some body parts twice.

Essential for Survival		Nonessential for Survival	
Heart	Pancreas	Arms	Ears
Lungs	Blood	Legs	Teeth
Brain	Nervous System	Eyes	Fingers
Liver	Skeleton	Gall Bladder	Hair

* If you choose to do Getting Started Option 2, list all 27 spiritual gift from page 9 of the book *Your Spiritual Gifts Can Help Your Church Grow* on a chalkboard or an overhead.

SECTION	60-MINUTE SESSION	90-MINUTE SESSION	ACTIVITY
GETTING STARTED	**10 MINUTES**	**20 MINUTES**	
Choice 1 *or*	10 Minutes	10 Minutes	The Body *or*
Choice 2			Primary and Essential Gifts
Option		10 Minutes	Gifts in Our Church
GETTING INTO THE WORD	**45 MINUTES**	**65 MINUTES**	
Step 1	25 Minutes	25 Minutes	The Knowing and Speaking Gifts
Step 2	20 Minutes	20 Minutes	The Serving and Miracle Gifts
Option		20 Minutes	Using the Gifts
GETTING PERSONAL	**5 MINUTES**	**5 MINUTES**	
	5 Minutes	5 Minutes	Ministry Through Gifts

SESSION PLAN

Leader's Choice

60- and 90-minute meeting options: This session is designed to be completed in one 60-minute meeting. If you want to extend the session to a 90-minute meeting, refer to the boxes marked with the clock symbol. These options will provide additional learning experiences expanding the session to 90 minutes.

Getting Started (10 Minutes)

Choice 1—The Body

As group members arrive, welcome them and hand each of them a 3x5-inch card on which is written a body part or organ. Have those with "Essential for Survival" body part or organ cards find others with "Essential for Survival" body part or organ cards. Have those with "Nonessential for Survival" body part or organ cards find others with "Nonessential for Survival" body part or organ cards. The group members will end up in two groups.

Explain: **Just as certain body parts or organs are essential for the survival of a person, so certain gifts from the Holy Spirit are essential for a healthy and**

growing church. We have studied these essential gifts—pastor, evangelist, apostle, leadership, administration, faith and exhortation. Of these gifts, Peter Wagner remarks, "The primary gift for local church growth is the gift of evangelist. The primary gift for the total health of the local church is the gift of pastor" (p. 189). Now there are many more gifts for the Body of Christ that are important and vital. We shall focus on those gifts in this session.

Choice 2—Primary and Essential Gifts

As everyone arrives have all 27 spiritual gifts listed on a chalkboard or an overhead. **Dr. Wagner has referred to certain gifts as primary and essential for local church health and growth. Other gifts he labels as supportive of these gifts. Just as a body cannot survive without certain organs, so the local church could not survive without these gifts. Everyone in the group has seven votes. I am going to call out each gift on this list of 27 gifts. Vote for the seven you feel are essential gifts for the local church.** After voting, compare the group's list to the list of pastor, apostle, evangelist, administration, faith, leadership and exhortation. **Now from this list of seven, which two gifts would you say are absolutely essential for the total health and growth of the local church?** After the group has discussed this, suggest that the choices for these two gifts are pastor and evangelist.

Getting Started Option (10 Minutes)

Gifts in Our Church

This option will add 10 minutes to either one of the Getting Started choices.
Of all the gifts on the list beyond these seven, have the group discuss:

* **Which gifts are most active in our church? Which are least active?**
* **Are there any gifts on this list that persons in the group might be uncomfortable with? Why?**

Getting into the Word (45 Minutes)

Step 1—Knowing and Speaking Gifts (25 Minutes)

Ten gifts are discussed in this chapter of *Your Spiritual Gifts Can Help Your Church Grow*. They are primarily found in 1 Corinthians 12 and Romans 12. Some of these gifts we are calling "knowing" (wisdom and knowledge) and "speaking" (prophecy, tongues and interpretation of tongues) gifts. The use of these gifts may be controversial in your church. Approach teaching about these gifts in a sensitive and informative manner.

Give everyone in the group a copy of the Session 10 handout, "Gifts for the Rest of the Body." Ask everyone to find a partner and then instruct the pairs to spend three to five minutes on Part One: The Knowing Gifts. Tell the pairs that all of those qualities that apply to reading and research pertain to the gift of knowledge. The qualities on the left-hand side under The Gift of Wisdom apply to the gift of wisdom.

Now instruct the pairs to complete Part Two: The Speaking Gifts and share with each other what they have written. Take about five minutes to do this.

Dr. Wagner points out that some churches believe that God does not speak directly to His people today except through inspired preaching. Others believe

that prophets speak forth today just as they did of old. The word prophet, *nabi*, means to be a mouthpiece for another, to speak forth. A prophet is both a forth-teller and a foreteller. To be anointed means to be empowered by the Holy Spirit.

✳ **What does our church believe about the gift of prophecy?**

✳ **Describe times when you have experienced the gift of prophecy.**

✳ **How does your position line up with Paul's teaching about prophecy in 1 Corinthians 14:1-5?**

The word vernacular means *common language.* **Now read 1 Corinthians 14:6-25.** Discuss:

✳ **How would you summarize Paul's experience of and teaching on tongues?**

✳ **What is our church's position on tongues and interpretation of tongues in worship?**

✳ **What functions or purposes do the speaking gifts serve in the Body of Christ?**

After the group discusses the speaking gifts, read the five functions which tongues serve found on page 205 of the book *Your Spiritual Gifts Can Help Your Church Grow.*

Step 2—The Serving and Miracle Gifts (20 Minutes)

Read to the group the definitions of the gifts of mercy, serving and helps.

"The gift of mercy is the special ability that God gives to certain members of the Body of Christ to feel genuine empathy and compassion for individuals, both Christian and non-Christian, who suffer distressing physical, mental or emotional problems, and to translate that compassion into cheerfully done deeds that reflect Christ's love and alleviate the suffering."

"The gift of helps is the special ability that God gives to some members of the Body of Christ to invest the talents they have in the life and ministry of other members of the Body, thus enabling the person helped to increase the effectiveness of his or her spiritual gifts."

"The gift of service is the special ability that God gives to certain members of the Body of Christ to identify the unmet needs involved in a task related to God's work, and to make use of available resources to meet those needs and help accomplish the desired goals."

Explain to the group: **The gift of mercy usually ministers to groups of people while the gift of helps may be more one-on-one. For example, the secretary who faithfully ministers to the pastor, Christian writer or scholar has the gift of helps. The Christian worker who organizes and runs a soup kitchen or clothing closet has the gift of mercy. The gift of service may be seen in many ways such as in the person who constantly repairs the homes of shut-ins or in the woman who prepares meals for the bereaved.**

On the chalkboard or overhead, list these three headings—"Mercy," "Helps" and "Service"—and ask the group to name ministries and/or persons within your church that demonstrate these gifts.

Now read the definitions of the gifts of healing and miracles.

"The gift of miracles is the special ability that God gives to certain members of the Body of Christ to serve as human intermediaries through whom it pleases God to perform powerful acts that are perceived by observers to have altered the ordinary course of nature."

"The gift of healing is the special ability that God gives to certain members of the Body of Christ to serve as human intermediaries through whom it pleases God to cure illness and restore health apart from the use of natural means."

Discuss:

* Has anyone witnessed or personally experienced healing or a miracle? Share your experiences.
* What purposes and functions do these gifts serve in the Body of Christ?

Some of the purposes and functions may be to build faith in the believers, to demonstrate God's power to unbelievers, and to restore and renew the Body of Christ.

Getting into the Word Option (20 Minutes)
Using the Gifts

This option will add 20 minutes to the Getting into the Word section.

Option 1—Identify within your group those who have the serving gifts. Have a time of prayer thanking God for them. Ask them to help you plan a project as a group that ministers beyond the group to others. It may be anything from preparing a meal for sick or shut-in people to repairing a home for someone in need.

Option 2—If you are in a congregation that allows the free expression of the speaking gifts, use this additional time for a time of ministry. Sing praise choruses. Worship. Have a time of prayer. As the Spirit leads, allow for tongues and interpretation, and for prophecy. Pray for those who wish to receive these gifts.

Pray for those who need healing and God's miraculous power in their lives.

Getting Personal (5 Minutes)
Ministry Through Gifts

Form a closing circle for prayer. If any group members have prayer requests concerning these gifts, invite them to share those requests. Ask group members to pray as they are led by God's Spirit. After a few minutes of prayer, close with a prayer like this: **Almighty God, we thank You for all the ministering and powerful gifts of the Holy Spirit. Show us how to use and minister these gifts to Your glory in Jesus' name. Amen.**

Gifts for the Rest of the Body

(CONTINUED ON
PAGE 79.)

Part One: The Knowing Gifts

The Gift of Knowledge
Definition: "The gift of knowledge is the special ability that God gives to certain members of the Body of Christ to discover, accumulate, analyze and clarify information and ideas that are pertinent to the growth and well-being of the Body."

Check the qualities you believe a person with the gift of knowledge might exhibit:

❑ enjoys studying and research

❑ bored with reading

❑ gets ideas in abundance from the Spirit

❑ enjoys socializing with people

❑ works well as a scholar

❑ has a poor memory

❑ is able to recall vast amounts of information

❑ short attention span

❑ eager to learn

Who are some people you know who may have this gift:

The Gifts of Wisdom
Definition: "The gift of wisdom is the special ability that God gives to certain members of the Body of Christ to know the mind of the Holy Spirit in such a way as to receive insight into how given knowledge may best be applied to specific needs arising in the Body of Christ."

What might you see as the qualities associated with this gift?
Put an X on the line where you see the strength of this gift.

_____
Gets to the heart of a problem quickly   Struggles with problems

_____
Enjoys working with people and their problems   Prefers working alone

_____
Makes correct decisions   Has trouble focusing
with surprising ease   on the problem or solution

Gifts for the Rest of the Body

Part Two: The Speaking Gifts

The Gift of Prophecy

(CONTINUED FROM
PAGE 77.)

Definition: "The gift of prophecy is the special ability that God gives to certain members of the Body of Christ to receive and communicate an immediate message of God to His people through a divinely anointed utterance."

The word prophecy means:

The word anointed means:

In our church the gift of prophecy is:

❑ encouraged   ❑ viewed only as inspired preaching

Read 1 Corinthians 14:1-5. Briefly paraphrase this teaching by Paul on prophecy:

The Gift of Tongues

Definition: "The gift of tongues is the special ability that God gives certain members of the Body of Christ (A) to speak to God in a language they have never learned and/or (B) to receive and communicate an immediate message of God to His people through a divinely anointed utterance in a language they have never learned."

Read Acts 2:1-21. How did God use tongues in this situation?

I believe that the gift of tongues is:

The Gift of Interpretation of Tongues

Definition: "The gift of interpretation of tongues is the special ability that God gives to certain members of the Body of Christ to make known in the vernacular the message of one who speaks in tongues."

Vernacular means:

I believe the interpretation of tongues is:

FIVE STEPS YOUR CHURCH CAN TAKE TO GROW THROUGH GIFTS

S E S S I O N   K E Y S

Key Verses

"Follow the way of love and eagerly desire spiritual gifts." 1 Corinthians 14:1

"Remember your leaders, who spoke the word of God to you. Consider the outcome of their way of life and imitate their faith." Hebrews 13:7

Key Idea

The gifts of the Holy Spirit are available to every church to grow numerically and spiritually.

Key Resources

* Chapter 10 of the book *Your Spiritual Gifts Can Help Your Church Grow*
* Copies of the Session 11 handout, "Unwrapping the Gifts"

Preparation

* Have Bibles, blank paper and pencils and pens for all group members who may need them.

Session **11** at a Glance

SECTION	60-MINUTE SESSION	90-MINUTE SESSION	ACTIVITY
GETTING STARTED	**10 MINUTES**	**20 MINUTES**	
Choice 1 *or*	10 Minutes	10 Minutes	The Key *or*
Choice 2			Do Not Be Ignorant
Option		10 Minutes	Involve Your Pastor
GETTING INTO THE WORD	**45 MINUTES**	**65 MINUTES**	
	45 Minutes	45 Minutes	Unwrapping the Gifts in Our Church
Option		20 Minutes	What Research Says
GETTING PERSONAL	**5 MINUTES**	**5 MINUTES**	
	5 Minutes	5 Minutes	Praying for Gifts

S E S S I O N   P L A N

Leader's Choice

60- and 90-minute meeting options: This session is designed to be completed in one 60-minute meeting. If you want to extend the session to a 90-minute meeting, refer to the boxes marked with the clock symbol. These options will provide additional learning experiences expanding the session to 90 minutes.

Getting Started (10 Minutes)

Choice 1—The Key

Warmly welcome everyone as they arrive and ask for a set of keys from each person. Put all the keys on a table in front of the group.

Keys are important. They open and unlock homes, cars, locks and numerous other things. Without our keys we would be stranded, dead in the water, going nowhere. Many churches face that problem. First of all, each of us has a set of keys—our spiritual gifts—that the Body of Christ needs for us to use to unlock God's power and ministry in our midst. Think of it. What if the pastors refused to use their keys or the teachers theirs? We could go nowhere. Now hold up each set of keys and let the group members identify their own keys. As each person takes back his or her keys, say **We thank God for your gifts.**

Not only does our church suffer when we do not use our keys—our gifts—there is also another person who holds the keys to growth and ministry in our church. If that person does not want gifts to function or your church to grow, that person can stop your church. Who holds the key? Have the group brainstorm and then read this quote from *Your Spiritual Gifts Can Help Your Church Grow:* "The pastor is God's key person for the growth of a local church, and if for some reason or other he or she is either indifferent or opposed to church growth or spiritual gifts, my advice is to postpone these five steps or they can easily backfire. I frankly hope that this book itself will help change the mind of many a reluctant pastor, but if it or other books, seminars or personal exhortation do not do the trick, continue to pray and wait for God's better timing." Discuss:

✳ **How open are we to spiritual gifts?**

✳ **How open is our leadership and pastor to spiritual gifts?**

Choice 2—Do Not Be Ignorant

As group members arrive, welcome them and put them in groups of three people each. Have each trio recall as many of the 27 spiritual gifts as it can. Give the trios paper and pencil to write down their lists. Call time in three minutes and list all the gifts the groups collectively had recalled. Then add to the list any that none of the groups remembered. Give the group that recalled the most spiritual gifts an ovation. Then read 1 Corinthians 12:1 and 14:1 to the group. Say, **The purpose of this study has been to remove our ignorance about spiritual gifts and to seek their use in our own lives and in our church. Peter Wagner suggests five steps for getting a church into the operation of spiritual gifts. In this session, we shall explore these steps together.**

Getting Started Option (10 Minutes)

Involve Your Pastor

This option will add 10 minutes to either one of the Getting Started choices.

If you are uncertain where your leadership or pastor stands on the operation of spiritual gifts in your church, invite your pastor to this session. Ask him or her what beliefs he or she has about spiritual gifts. Invite your pastor to participate in this study so that together the group and your pastor may see what steps are suggested for getting a church into the operation of the gifts of the Spirit.

Getting into the Word (45 Minutes)

Unwrapping the Gifts in Our Church

The purpose of this session is to walk your group through the five steps for putting spiritual gifts to work in your congregation. Since your pastor is the key to this happening, it would be most effective for him or her to be with you in this process. If gifts are already operating in your church and you desire to deepen their utilization in your group, then the pastor's presence would be less important. As each step is studied, first write it on a chalkboard or an overhead.

Step 1—Agree on a Philosophy of Ministry

Give each person in the group a piece of paper and pencil. Ask each person to write down God's purpose for your congregation. Then write down the gifts you believe are necessary for accomplishing God's purpose. As each person is doing this, be certain that the list of all 27 gifts is in front of the group on a chalkboard or an overhead. Bring everyone back together after about seven minutes and invite everyone to read his or her purpose statement. As they read, list on the board different statements. Next, work together as a group until you have your church purpose statement down to one concise sentence. Then discuss:

✳ **Which spiritual gifts do we expect God to give us to accomplish His purpose for us?**

Circle those gifts on your list that the group can agree upon as needing to be operative in your church.

✳ **Are we open to the sign gifts, such as tongues, miracles, prophecy and healing? Are they to be used in public worship or only in small-group settings?**

✳ **What do we believe about the baptism of the Holy Spirit? Do we believe tongues to be the evidence of the baptism of the Holy Spirit?**

✳ **How do we treat people new to our fellowship or within our church who have different views on gifts than we do?**

✳ **Can we make a covenant with one another not to fight over what we believe about the Holy Spirit and gifts?**

Have everyone read aloud Ephesians 4:1-7 in unison.

Step 2—Initiate a Growth Process

As a group, discuss ways that your congregation can begin to identify gifts among your people, train and equip those gifted people for ministry and then release them for ministry. Write these three categories on the board: "Identify," "Train and Equip" and "Release."

As a group, brainstorm under each category what might be necessary to mobilize that gifting. For example, various Sunday School classes or small groups could study and discover their spiritual gifts as you have. You might mobilize a team of volunteers who would screen those people and interview them. The volunteers then might be directed to train these gifted people within or beyond your church to help each of them utilize their spiritual gifts. Training might include evangelism techniques, hospital and shut-in visitation, or working in the stewardship and budget ministry of your church. Spend about 10 minutes brainstorming the needs you have for spiritual gifts and how to direct those needs to being equipped and used in your church.

Step 3—Structure for Gifts and Growth

Invite your pastor to review for you the structures that already exist in your church for using spiritual gifts and helping your church to grow. Read Hebrews 13:7. Remember, the pastor is the key for growth and utilizing gifts within your church. Discuss:

✳ **Does our church genuinely follow the leaders and pastor?**

✳ **How does our church handle issues of authority?**

✳ **What kinds of attitudes exist in our church toward the pastor and leadership?**

Step 4—Unwrap the Spiritual Gifts

Give everyone a copy of the Session 11 handout, "Unwrapping the Gifts." Divide up into pairs and discuss how your church might approach each step suggested. After five to seven minutes, return to the total group and share what every pair has discussed.

Step 5—Expect God's Blessing

Discuss:

* **What do we expect God to do in our midst in the coming months and years?**
* **What commitment do we need from each of us to realize God's blessing?**

Getting into the Word Option (20 Minutes)

What Research Says

This option will add 20 minutes to the Getting into the Word section.

Tell the group that research has indicated that in many churches, 85 percent of the time is spent in administration while only 15 percent is spent in ministry. Evaluate all the time your church spends in administrative functions and in ministry. Discuss:

* **How much time on a monthly basis do we do administration?**
* **How much time do we spend in ministry?**
* **How many volunteers do we have in doing ministry? Some believe that the 80/20 formula applies to churches as well as businesses. In other words, 20 percent of the people give 80 percent of the money and do 80 percent of the ministry.**
* **Is this true of our church? How would the proper use of spiritual gifts help this ratio in our church?**

Getting Personal (5 Minutes)

Praying for Gifts

Have a time of prayer in the total group. Lead a guided prayer for the following items. Encourage people to pray aloud as they are led while everyone prays silently with them.

Let us come to our heavenly Father and pray for: our church, our pastor, our leaders, the stirring up of spiritual gifts in our midst, unity in our church, our church to grow and our church to reach the lost for Jesus Christ.

Unwrapping the Gifts

Below each statement, list as many ways as you can think of that each item might be implemented in your church.

1. Motivate the congregation from the pulpit.

2. Study the biblical teaching on gifts.

3. Help people discover their gifts.

4. Sponsor a spiritual-gifts workshop.

5. Set a schedule for accountability.

6. Continue the experience indefinitely.

SESSION 12

FIND YOUR GIFTS

SESSION KEYS

Key Verse

"Speaking the truth in love, we will in all things grow up into him who is the Head, that is, Christ. From him the whole body, joined and held together by every supporting ligament, grows and builds itself up in love, as each part does its work." Ephesians 4:15,16

Key Idea

God has given gifts to believers in the Body of Christ by the Holy Spirit to empower and equip the Body to do ministry in the world.

Key Resources

* Chapter 11 of the book *Your Spiritual Gifts Can Help Your Church Grow*
* Copies of the "Wagner-Modified Houts Questionnaire"

Preparation

* Have Bibles, blank paper and pencils and pens for all group members who may need them.
* Write one spiritual gift on 27 different adhesive labels. If your group has less than 27 people then give two or more adhesive labels to some people.
* Have poster board, felt-tip pens, construction paper and glue for group members.

Session 12 at a Glance

SECTION	60-MINUTE SESSION	90-MINUTE SESSION	ACTIVITY
GETTING STARTED	10 MINUTES	20 MINUTES	
	10 Minutes	10 Minutes	The Spiritual Gifts
Option		10 Minutes	Listing the Gifts
GETTING INTO THE WORD	45 MINUTES	65 MINUTES	
Step 1	20 Minutes	20 Minutes	Summarizing the Gifts
Step 2	25 Minutes	25 Minutes	Taking the Gifts Survey
Option		20 Minutes	Sharing About My Gifts
GETTING PERSONAL	5 MINUTES	5 MINUTES	
	5 Minutes	5 Minutes	Thanking God for Our Gifts

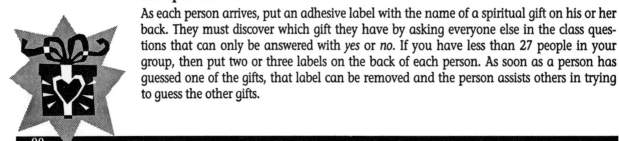

S E S S I O N   P L A N

Leader's Choice

60- and 90-minute meeting options: This session is designed to be completed in one 60-minute meeting. If you want to extend the session to a 90-minute meeting, refer to the boxes marked with the clock symbol. These options will provide additional learning experiences expanding the session to 90 minutes.

Getting Started (10 Minutes)

The Spiritual Gifts

As each person arrives, put an adhesive label with the name of a spiritual gift on his or her back. They must discover which gift they have by asking everyone else in the class questions that can only be answered with *yes* or *no*. If you have less than 27 people in your group, then put two or three labels on the back of each person. As soon as a person has guessed one of the gifts, that label can be removed and the person assists others in trying to guess the other gifts.

Getting Started Option (10 Minutes)

Listing the Gifts

This option will add 10 minutes to the Getting Started activity.

After each person has guessed all of the gifts he or she had on his or her back, then put all of the labels on a big table. Tell the group that they are going to sort the gifts according to category. Let them come up with three or four different categories they believe the gifts could be organized into, i.e. sign gifts, speaking gifts, serving gifts, leadership gifts, etc. As a group, put the labels into those groupings with people giving reasons why they would assign a gift to one category and not another.

Getting into the Word (45 Minutes)

Step 1—Summarizing the Gifts (20 Minutes)

Divide the total group into three small groups. Assign each small group one of the following Scripture passages: Romans 12:1-8; 1 Corinthians 12:1-11; Ephesians 4:1-16.

Each group is to take their poster board, felt-tip pens, construction paper and glue, and make a poster that summarizes the gifts and teaching of its passage. Each group has 10 minutes to make its poster.

After the groups have finished, ask each small group to show its poster to the total group and explain what it means.

Step 2—Taking the Gifts Survey (25 Minutes)

Pass out copies of the questionnaire. Invite everyone in the group to take the questionnaire. After all have completed the questionnaire on spiritual gifts, explain the scoring. When everyone is confident about how he or she scored, ask people in the group to share their primary gifts.

Getting into the Word Option (20 Minutes)

Sharing About My Gifts

This option will add 20 minutes to the Getting into the Word section.

Divide up into pairs or trios. Invite the partners to share with one another:

* **What surprised me about my gift(s) was:**
* **What reassures me about my gift(s) is:**
* **One way I want to use my gift(s) in the future is:**

Getting Personal (5 Minutes)

Thanking God for Our Gifts

Have everyone get with a partner to pray. Before the partners pray for one another, invite them to share with each other what needs they have pertaining to their spiritual gifts.

Gather the total group. Form a circle. Ask each person in the group (beginning with you) to pray aloud for the person on his or her right thanking God for one of the gifts that person has. Go around the circle to the right and pray.

Name _____ Date _____

Wagner-Modified Houts Questionnaire

Greetings!

You are about to become involved in an exciting spiritual exercise. God has given you one or more spiritual gifts if you are a Christian, and discovering that gift or gifts will be a thrilling experience.

You will be asked to answer the 125 questions found in the "Wagner-Modified Houts Questionnaire." This spiritual gifts discovery instrument was originally suggested by Dr. Richard F. Houts in 1976. Subsequently, I modified it and included it in my book *Your Spiritual Gifts Can Help Your Church Grow*—now the best-selling book in the field of spiritual gifts. The copy you have in your hand is the seventh edition and the first complete revision of the original published version.

Thousands and thousands of believers have been blessed by taking the Wagner-Modified Houts Questionnaire. Constant feedback from them has enabled us to refine it to the point where it will give you a fairly accurate picture of what kind of ministry God expects you to be carrying out in your group of believers.

However, do not regard the results of this test as final. The three or four gifts on which you score highest may or may not be your real spiritual gifts. Nevertheless, you can be sure that it will be worthwhile to pray about and begin to experiment with those particular gifts. Be sure to seek the counsel of other Christians around you as you experiment so that they will help you confirm what gifts you do have. If you are under 25 years of age or if you have been a Christian for less than six months, treat the results of this questionnaire a bit more tentatively than otherwise because the questions are based on actual past experiences.

C. Peter Wagner
Fuller Theological Seminary

Before You Start...

Follow these four steps...

Step 1 Go through the list of 125 statements in the questionnaire on pages 97-107. For each one, mark to what extent the statement is true of your life: MUCH, SOME, LITTLE, or NOT AT ALL.

Warning! Do not score according to what you think should be true or hope might be true in the future. Be honest and score on the basis of past experience. If you are a young Christian or new in the faith, the results will need extra care in interpretation.

Step 2 When you are finished, score the questionnaire by means of the Wagner-Modified Houts Chart on page 109.

Step 3 After filling in your scores, refer to pages 111-117 for the definitions of the spiritual gifts. You will want to study the gift definitions and Scripture references.

Step 4 Complete the exercises on page 119 to gain a tentative evaluation of where your gifts may lie and to explore the implications for your ministry in the Body of Christ.

STEP 1: Wagner-Modified Houts Questionnaire

For each statement, mark to what extent it is true of your life:
MUCH, SOME, LITTLE, or NOT AT ALL.

(3) MUCH	(2) SOME	(1) LITTLE	(0) NOT AT ALL

_____ 1. I have a desire to speak direct messages from God that edify, exhort or comfort others.

_____ 2. I have enjoyed relating to a certain group of people over a long period of time, sharing personally in their successes and their failures.

_____ 3. People have told me that I have helped them learn biblical truth in a meaningful way.

_____ 4. I have applied spiritual truth effectively to situations in my own life.

_____ 5. Others have told me I have helped them distinguish key and important facts of Scripture.

_____ 6. I have verbally encouraged the wavering, the troubled or the discouraged.

_____ 7. Others in the church have noted that I was able to see through phoniness before it was evident to other people.

_____ 8. I find I manage money well in order to give liberally to the Lord's work.

_____ 9. I have assisted Christian leaders to relieve them for their essential job.

_____ 10. I have a desire to work with those who have physical or mental problems, to alleviate their suffering.

_____ 11. I feel comfortable relating to ethnics and minorities, and they seem to accept me.

_____ 12. I have led others to a decision for salvation through faith in Christ.

_____ 13. My home is always open to people passing through who need a place to stay.

_____ 14. When in a group, I am the one others often look to for vision and direction.

_____ 15. When I speak, people seem to listen and agree.

_____ 16. When a group I am in is lacking organization, I tend to step in to fill the gap.

_____ 17. Others can point to specific instances where my prayers have resulted in visible miracles.

_____ 18. In the name of the Lord, I have been used in curing diseases instantaneously.

_____ 19. I have spoken in tongues.

_____ 20. Sometimes when a person speaks in tongues, I get an idea about what God is saying.

_____ 21. I could live more comfortably, but I choose not to in order to live with the poor.

_____ 22. I am single and enjoy it.

_____ 23. I spend at least an hour a day in prayer.

_____ 24. I have spoken to evil spirits and they have obeyed me.

_____ 25. I enjoy being called upon to do special jobs around the church.

_____ 26. Through God I have revealed specific things that will happen in the future.

_____ 27. I have enjoyed assuming the responsibility for the spiritual well-being of a particular group of Christians.

_____ 28. I feel I can explain the New Testament teaching about the health and ministry of the Body of Christ in a relevant way.

_____ 29. I can intuitively arrive at solutions to fairly complicated problems.

_____ 30. I have had insights of spiritual truth that others have said helped bring them closer to God.

_____ 31. I can effectively motivate people to get involved in ministry when it is needed.

_____ 32. I can "see" the Spirit of God resting on certain people from time to time.

_____ 33. My giving records show that I give considerably more than 10 percent of my income to the Lord's work.

_____ 34. Other people have told me that I have helped them become more effective in their ministries.

_____ 35. I have cared for others when they have had material or physical needs.

_____ 36. I feel I could learn another language well in order to minister to those in a different culture.

_____ 37. I have shared joyfully how Christ has brought me to Himself in a way that is meaningful to nonbelievers.

_____ 38. I enjoy taking charge of church suppers or social events.

_____ 39. I have believed God for the impossible and seen it happen in a tangible way.

_____ 40. Other Christians have followed my leadership because they believed in me.

_____ 41. I enjoy handling the details of organizing ideas, people, resources and time for more effective ministry.

_____ 42. God has used me personally to perform supernatural signs and wonders.

_____ 43. I enjoy praying for sick people because I know that many of them will be healed as a result.

_____ 44. I have spoken an immediate message of God to His people in a language I have never learned.

_____ 45. I have interpreted tongues with the result that the Body of Christ was edified, exhorted or comforted.

_____ 46. Living a simple lifestyle is an exciting challenge for me.

_____ 47. Other people have noted that I feel more indifferent about not being married than most.

_____ 48. When I hear a prayer request, I pray for that need for several days at least.

_____ 49. I have actually heard a demon speak in a loud voice.

_____ 50. I don't have many special skills, but I do what needs to be done around the church.

_____ 51. People have told me that I have communicated timely and urgent messages that must have come directly from the Lord.

_____ 52. I feel unafraid of giving spiritual guidance and direction in a group of Christians.

_____ 53. I can devote considerable time to learning new biblical truths in order to communicate them to others.

_____ 54. When a person has a problem I can frequently guide them to the best Biblical solution.

_____ 55. Through study or experience I have discerned major strategies or techniques God seems to use in furthering His kingdom.

_____ 56. People have come to me in their afflictions or suffering, and told me that they have been helped, relieved and healed.

_____ 57. I can tell with a fairly high degree of assurance when a person is afflicted by an evil spirit.

_____ 58. When I am moved by an appeal to give to God's work, I usually can find the money I need to do it.

_____ 59. I have enjoyed doing routine tasks that led to more effective ministry by others.

_____ 60. I enjoy visiting in hospitals and/or retirement homes, and feel I do well in such a ministry.

_____ 61. People of a different race or culture have been attracted to me, and we have related well.

_____ 62. Non-Christians have noted that they feel comfortable when they are around me, and that I have a positive effect on them toward developing a faith in Christ.

_____ 63. When people come to our home, they indicate that they "feel at home" with us.

_____ 64. Other people have told me that I had faith to accomplish what seemed impossible to them.

_____ 65. When I set goals, others seem to accept them readily.

_____ 66. I have been able to make effective and efficient plans for accomplishing the goals of a group.

_____ 67. God regularly seems to do impossible things through my life.

_____ 68. Others have told me that God healed them of an emotional problem when I ministered to them.

_____ 69. I can speak to God in a language I have never learned.

_____ 70. I have prayed that I may interpret if someone begins speaking in tongues.

_____ 71. I am not poor, but I can identify with poor people.

_____ 72. I am glad I have more time to serve the Lord because I am single.

_____ 73. Intercessory prayer is one of my favorite ways of spending time.

_____ 74. Others call on me when they suspect that someone is demonized.

_____ 75. Others have mentioned that I seem to enjoy routine tasks and do well at them.

_____ 76. I sometimes have a strong sense of what God wants to say to people in response to a particular situation.

_____ 77. I have helped fellow believers by guiding them to relevant portions of the Bible and praying with them.

_____ 78. I feel I can communicate biblical truths to others and see resulting changes in knowledge, attitudes, values or conduct.

_____ 79. Some people indicate that I have perceived and applied biblical truth to the specific needs of fellow believers.

_____ 80. I study and read quite a bit in order to learn new biblical truths.

_____ 81. I have a desire to effectively counsel the perplexed, the guilty or the addicted.

_____ 82. I can recognize whether a person's teaching is from God, from Satan, or of human origin.

_____ 83. I am so confident that God will meet my needs that I give to Him sacrificially and consistently.

_____ 84. When I do things behind the scenes and others are helped, I am joyful.

_____ 85. People call on me to help those who are less fortunate.

_____ 86. I would be willing to leave comfortable surroundings if it would enable me to share Christ with more people.

_____ 87. I get frustrated when others don't seem to share their faith with unbelievers as much as I do.

_____ 88. Others have mentioned to me that I am a very hospitable person.

_____ 89. There have been times when I have felt sure I knew God's specific will for the future growth of His work, even when others have not been so sure.

_____ 90. When I join a group, others seem to back off and expect me to take the leadership.

_____ 91. I am able to give directions to others without using persuasion to get them to accomplish a task.

_____ 92. People have told me that I was God's instrument which brought supernatural change in lives or circumstances.

_____ 93. I have prayed for others and physical healing has actually occurred.

_____ 94. When I give a public message in tongues, I expect it to be interpreted.

_____ 95. I have interpreted tongues in a way that seemed to bless others.

_____ 96. Others tell me I sacrifice much materially in order to minister.

_____ 97. I am single and have little difficulty controlling my sexual desires.

_____ 98. Others have told me that my prayers for them have been answered in tangible ways.

_____ 99. Other people have been instantly delivered from demonic oppression when I have prayed.

_____ 100. I prefer being active and doing something rather than just sitting around talking or reading or listening to a speaker.

_____ 101. I sometimes feel that I know exactly what God wants to do in ministry at a specific point in time.

_____ 102. People have told me that I have helped them be restored to the Christian community.

_____ 103. Studying the Bible and sharing my insights with others is very satisfying for me.

_____ 104. I have felt an unusual presence of God and personal confidence when important decisions needed to be made.

_____ 105. I have the ability to discover new truths for myself through reading or observing situations firsthand.

_____ 106. I have urged others to seek a biblical solution to their affliction or suffering.

_____ 107. I can tell whether a person speaking in tongues is genuine.

_____ 108. I have been willing to maintain a lower standard of living in order to benefit God's work.

_____ 109. When I serve the Lord, I really don't care who gets the credit.

_____ 110. I would enjoy spending time with a lonely, shut-in person or someone in prison.

_____ 111. More than most, I have had a strong desire to see peoples of other countries won to the Lord.

_____ 112. I am attracted to nonbelievers because of my desire to win them to Christ.

_____ 113. I have desired to make my home available to those in the Lord's service whenever needed.

_____ 114. Others have told me that I am a person of unusual vision, and I agree.

_____ 115. When I am in charge, things seem to run smoothly.

_____ 116. I have enjoyed bearing the responsibility for the success of a particular task within my church.

_____ 117. In the name of the Lord, I have been able to recover sight to the blind.

_____ 118. When I pray for the sick, either I or they feel sensations of tingling or warmth.

_____ 119. When I speak in tongues, I believe it is edifying to the Lord's Body.

_____ 120. I have interpreted tongues in such a way that the message appeared to be directly from God.

_____ 121. Poor people accept me because I choose to live on their level.

_____ 122. I readily identify with Paul's desire for others to be single as he was.

_____ 123. When I pray, God frequently speaks to me, and I recognize His voice.

_____ 124. I cast out demons in Jesus' name.

_____ 125. I respond cheerfully when asked to do a job, even if it seems menial.

Step 2: Wagner-Modified Houts Chart

In the grid below, enter the numerical value of each of your responses next to the number of the corresponding statement from **Step 1**.

MUCH = 3   SOME = 2   LITTLE = 1   NOT AT ALL = 0

Then add up the five numbers that you have recorded in each row and place the sum in the "Total" column.

VALUE OF ANSWERS					TOTAL	GIFT (see pp. 111-117)
1	26	51	76	101		A. Prophecy
2	27	52	77	102		B. Pastor
3	28	53	78	103		C. Teaching
4	29	54	79	104		D. Wisdom
5	30	55	80	105		E. Knowledge
6	31	56	81	106		F. Exhortation
7	32	57	82	107		G. Discerning of Spirits
8	33	58	83	108		H. Giving
9	34	59	84	109		I. Helps
10	35	60	85	110		J. Mercy
11	36	61	86	111		K. Missionary
12	37	62	87	112		L. Evangelist
13	38	63	88	113		M. Hospitality
14	39	64	89	114		N. Faith
15	40	65	90	115		O. Leadership
16	41	66	91	116		P. Administration
17	42	67	92	117		Q. Miracles
18	43	68	93	118		R. Healing
19	44	69	94	119		S. Tongues
20	45	70	95	120		T. Interpretation
21	46	71	96	121		U. Voluntary Poverty
22	47	72	97	122		V. Celibacy
23	48	73	98	123		W. Intercession
24	49	74	99	124		X. Exorcism
25	50	75	100	125		Y. Service

Step 3: Review Gift Definitions and Scripture References

This and the following 3 pages contain **suggested** definitions of the spiritual gifts. While not meant to be dogmatic or final, these definitions and supporting Scriptures do correspond to characteristics of the gifts as expressed in the *Wagner-Modified Houts Questionnaire.*

A. Prophecy. The gift of prophecy is the special ability that God gives to certain members of the Body of Christ to receive and communicate an immediate message of God to His people through a divinely anointed utterance.
1 Cor. 12:10,28   Eph. 4:11-14   Rom. 12:6
Luke 7:26   Acts 15:32   Acts 21:9-11

B. Pastor. The gift of pastor is the special ability that God gives to certain members of the Body of Christ to assume a long-term personal responsibility for the spiritual welfare of a group of believers.
Eph. 4:11-14   1 Tim. 3:1-7   John 10:1-18   1 Pet. 5:1-3

C. Teaching. The gift of teaching is the special ability that God gives to certain members of the Body of Christ to communicate information relevant to the health and ministry of the Body and its members in such a way that others will learn.
1 Cor. 12:28   Eph. 4:11-14   Rom. 12:7
Acts 18:24-28   Acts 20:20,21

D. Wisdom. The gift of wisdom is the special ability that God gives to certain members of the Body of Christ to know the mind of the Holy Spirit in such a way as to receive insight into how given knowledge may best be applied to specific needs arising in the Body of Christ.
1 Cor. 2:1-13   1 Cor. 12:8   Acts 6:3,10
Jas. 1:5,6   2 Pet. 3:15,16

E. Knowledge. The gift of knowledge is the special ability that God gives to certain members of the Body of Christ to discover, accumulate, analyze, and clarify information and ideas which are pertinent to the well-being of the Body.
1 Cor. 2:14   1 Cor. 12:8   Acts 5:1-11
Col. 2:2,3   2 Cor. 11:6

F. Exhortation. The gift of exhortation is the special ability that God gives to certain members of the Body of Christ to minister words of comfort, consolation, encouragement, and counsel to other members of the Body in such a way that they feel helped and healed.
Rom. 12:8   1 Tim. 4:13   Heb. 10:25   Acts 14:22

G. Discerning of Spirits. The gift of discerning of spirits is the special ability that God gives to certain members of the Body of Christ to know with assurance whether certain behavior purported to be of God is in reality divine, human or satanic.

1 Cor. 12:10   Acts 5:1-11   Acts 16:16-18
1 John 4:1-6   Matt. 16:21-23

H. Giving. The gift of giving is the special ability that God gives to certain members of the Body of Christ to contribute their material resources to the work of the Lord with liberality and cheerfulness.

Rom. 12:8   2 Cor. 8:1-7   2 Cor. 9:2-8   Mark 12:41-44

I. Helps. The gift of helps is the special ability that God gives to certain members of the Body of Christ to invest the talents they have in the life and ministry of other members of the Body, with thus enabling those others to increase the effectiveness of their own spiritual gifts.

1 Cor. 12:28   Rom. 16:1,2   Acts 9:36
Luke 8:2,3   Mark 15:40,41

J. Mercy. The gift of mercy is the special ability that God gives to certain members of the Body of Christ to feel genuine empathy and compassion for individuals (both Christian and non-Christian) who suffer distressing physical, mental or emotional problems, and to translate that compassion into cheerfully done deeds that reflect Christ's love and alleviate the suffering.

Rom. 12:8   Mark 9:41   Acts 16:33,34   Luke 10:33-35
Matt. 20:29-34   Matt. 25:34-40   Acts 11:28-30

K. Missionary. The gift of missionary is the special ability that God gives to certain members of the Body of Christ to minister whatever other spiritual gifts they have in a second culture.

1 Cor. 9:19-23   Acts 8:4   Acts 13:2,3
Acts 22:21   Rom. 10:15

L. Evangelist. The gift of evangelist is the special ability that God gives to certain members of the Body of Christ to share the gospel with unbelievers in such a way that men and women become Jesus' disciples and responsible members of the Body of Christ.

Eph. 4:11-14   2 Tim. 4:5   Acts 8:5,6
Acts 8:26-40   Acts 14:21   Acts 21:8

M. Hospitality. The gift of hospitality is the special ability that God gives to certain members of the Body of Christ to provide an open house and a warm welcome to those in need of food and lodging.

1 Pet. 4:9   Rom. 12:9-13   Rom. 16:23
Acts 16:14,15   Heb. 13:1,2

N. Faith. The gift of faith is the special ability that God gives to certain members of the Body of Christ to discern with extraordinary confidence the will and purposes of God for his work.

1 Cor. 12:9   Acts 11:22-24   Acts 27:21-25
Heb. 11   Rom. 4:18-21

O. Leadership. The gift of leadership is the special ability that God gives to certain members of the Body of Christ to set goals in accordance with God's purpose for the future and to communicate these goals to others in such a way that they voluntarily and harmoniously work together to accomplish those goals for the glory of God.

1 Tim. 5:17   Acts 7:10   Acts 15:7-11
Rom. 12:8   Heb. 13:17   Luke 9:51

FIND YOUR
GIFTS

QUESTIONNAIRE

P. Administration. The gift of administration is the special ability that God gives to certain members of the Body of Christ to understand clearly the immediate and long-range goals of a particular unit of the Body of Christ and to devise and execute effective plans for the accomplishment of those goals.

1 Cor. 12:28   Acts 6:1-7   Acts 27:11
Luke 14:28-30   Titus 1:5

Q. Miracles. The gift of miracles is the special ability that God gives to certain members of the Body of Christ to serve as human intermediaries through whom it pleases God to perform powerful acts that are perceived by observers to have altered the ordinary course of nature.

1 Cor. 12:10,28 Acts 9:36-42   Acts 19:11-20
Acts 20:7-12   Rom. 15:18,19   2 Cor. 12:12

R. Healing. The gift of healing is the special ability that God gives to certain members of the Body of Christ to serve as human intermediaries through whom it pleases God to cure illness and restore health apart from the use of natural means.

1 Cor. 12:9,28   Acts 3:1-10   Acts 5:12-16
Acts 9:32-35   Acts 28:7-10

S. Tongues. The gift of tongues is the special ability that God gives to certain members of the Body of Christ (a) to speak to God in a language they have never learned and/or (b) to receive and communicate an immediate message of God to His people through a divinely anointed utterance in a language they never learned.

1 Cor. 12:10,28 1 Cor. 14:13-19 Acts 2:1-13
Acts 10:44-46   Acts 19:1-7   Mark 16:17

T. Interpretation. The gift of interpretation is the special ability that God gives to certain members of the Body of Christ to make known in the vernacular the message of one who speaks in tongues.

1 Cor. 12:10,30 1 Cor. 14:13   1 Cor. 14:26-28

U. Voluntary Poverty. The gift of voluntary poverty is the special ability that God gives to certain members of the Body of Christ to renounce material comfort and luxury and adopt a personal lifestyle equivalent to those living at the poverty level in a given society in order to serve God more effectively.

1 Cor. 13:1-3   Acts 2:44,45   Acts 4:34-37
2 Cor. 6:10   2 Cor. 8:9

© 1995 by Gospel Light. Permission to photocopy granted for classroom use only.   115

V. Celibacy. The gift of celibacy is the special ability that God gives to certain members of the Body of Christ to remain single and enjoy it; to be unmarried and not suffer undue sexual temptations.
1 Cor. 7:7,8   Matt. 19:10-12

W. Intercession. The gift of intercession is the special ability that God gives to certain members of the Body of Christ to pray for extended periods of time on a regular basis and see frequent and specific answers to their prayers, to a degree much greater than that which is expected of the average Christian.
Jas. 5:14-16   1 Tim. 2:1,2   Col. 1:9-12
Col. 4:12,13   Acts 12:12   Luke 22:41-44

X. Exorcism. The gift of exorcism is the special ability that God gives to certain members of the Body of Christ to cast out demons and evil spirits.
Matt. 12:22-32   Luke 10:12-20   Acts 8:5-8   Acts 16:16-18

Y. Service. The gift of service is the special ability that God gives to certain members of the Body of Christ to identify the unmet needs involved in a task related to God's work, and to make use of available resources to meet those needs and help accomplish the desired results.
2 Tim. 1:16-18   Rom. 12:7   Acts 6:1-7
Titus 3:14   Gal. 6:2,10

Step 4: Gifts and Ministries

1. Using the results of the Wagner-Modified Houts Chart on page 109, enter below in the "Dominant" section your three highest-rated gifts. Then enter in the "Subordinate" section the next three highest-scoring gifts. This will give you a *tentative* evaluation of where your gifts may lie.

Dominant:

1.

2.

3.

Subordinate:

1.

2.

3.

2. What ministries are you **now** performing (formally or informally) in the Body?

3. Are there any of these ministries that you are not especially gifted for? God may be calling you to consider changes.

4. Is your vocational status lay or clergy?

5. In light of your gift cluster and vocational status, what are some ministry models or roles suitable for you? What specific roles has God possibly gifted you for in the Body of Christ?